MICROSOFT WORD

FOR BEGINNERS *2023*

BUILDING YOUR WRITING AND DOCUMENT
CREATION SKILLS

by

MARY LAMBERTH

COPYRIGHT

Printed in the United States of America

© 2023 by Mary Lamberth

New Age Publishing

USA | UK | CANADA

TABLE OF CONTENTS

CONCLUSION

INTRODUCTION

Welcome to this practical guide to **MICROSOFT WORD FOR BEGINNERS**. I am happy to be your guide as I help you in this introductory tutorial to become an expert on Microsoft Word. We'll cover all the basic features and functionalities in the software while at the same time exploring the new interface of Microsoft Word.

Some of the features we will cover, although not exclusively these, are:

- Formatting text in Microsoft Word. These include looking at the features, fonts, and colors accompanying it.
- Inserting images in Microsoft Word. We will also cover image editing as well.
- Creating tables in Microsoft Word.
- Document preparation before letting the public view it as well as printing documents.

Remember that this guide is meant to be interactive. That means it should be followed as something other than a textbook. When you read a manual or feature, you learn when you practice it. So, make sure you have your Microsoft Word open as you read this guide.

We'll start this guide with the start screen on Microsoft Word.

PART ONE GETTING STARTED WITH MICROSOFT WORD

This chapter will cover the basics of opening a file, understanding the **start screen**, and navigating through an opened document. Along the way, you will understand the different commands and command groups and the tabs you can find on the ribbon.

START SCREEN

When you open up your Microsoft Word software, the first screen is the **start screen** like below.

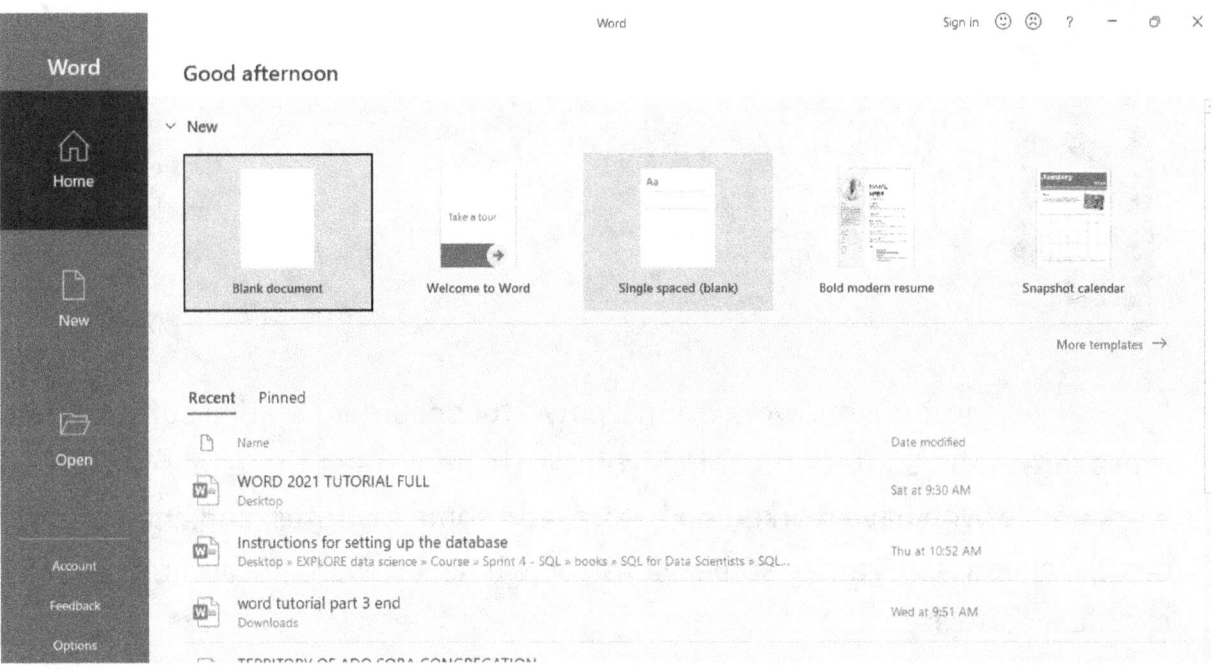

This start screen is similar to other Microsoft products like PowerPoint and Excel. Microsoft wants its products to be harmonious with users so first-time users will be comfortable using them.

The start screen is like a one-stop shop that helps us to interact with all the functionalities you can get in Microsoft Word. It offers lots of things you can do here. But let me point out three significant icons you should notice.

If you look at the image of the start screen above again, you will notice three ubiquitous icons on the left. The first is the **Home tab**. You can see that I have already selected it. That is the tab I am currently navigating on. Below the home tab is the **New tab**. After that is the **Open tab**.

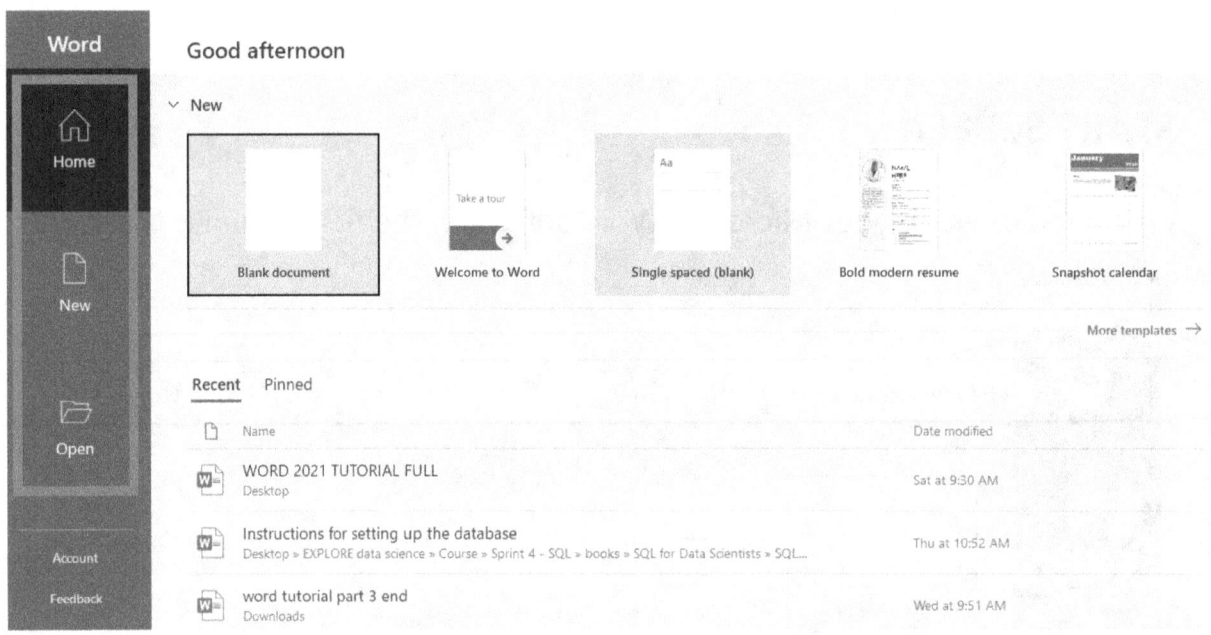

You can get most of your work on this powerful document editing software between these three tabs. Some of the things you can do from these three tabs are to find files, work on files you have worked on before, add some favorites, and, interestingly, you can go ahead and gather some ideas for what you want to accomplish with this excellent software.

Home Tab

So, right now, we're on the Home tab. If you watch the screen on the Home tab, you can find some things you can do here. We can start a new document, such as a blank document. I'll demonstrate that in a few minutes. We can also check out this **Welcome to Word** tutorial provided you want to.

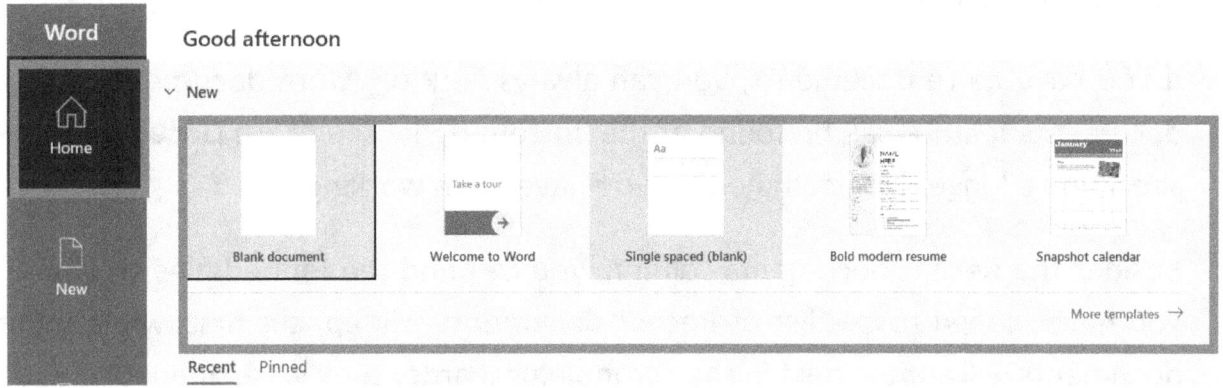

Besides all these, you can also look at some of the templates Microsoft offers. A template is a document that creates a copy of itself when you open it. We'll look at some excellent templates on Microsoft Word. That is when we visit the **New tab**.

If we move down below on the Home tab, we can find other things to do. For example, you can take a look at your recent activity.

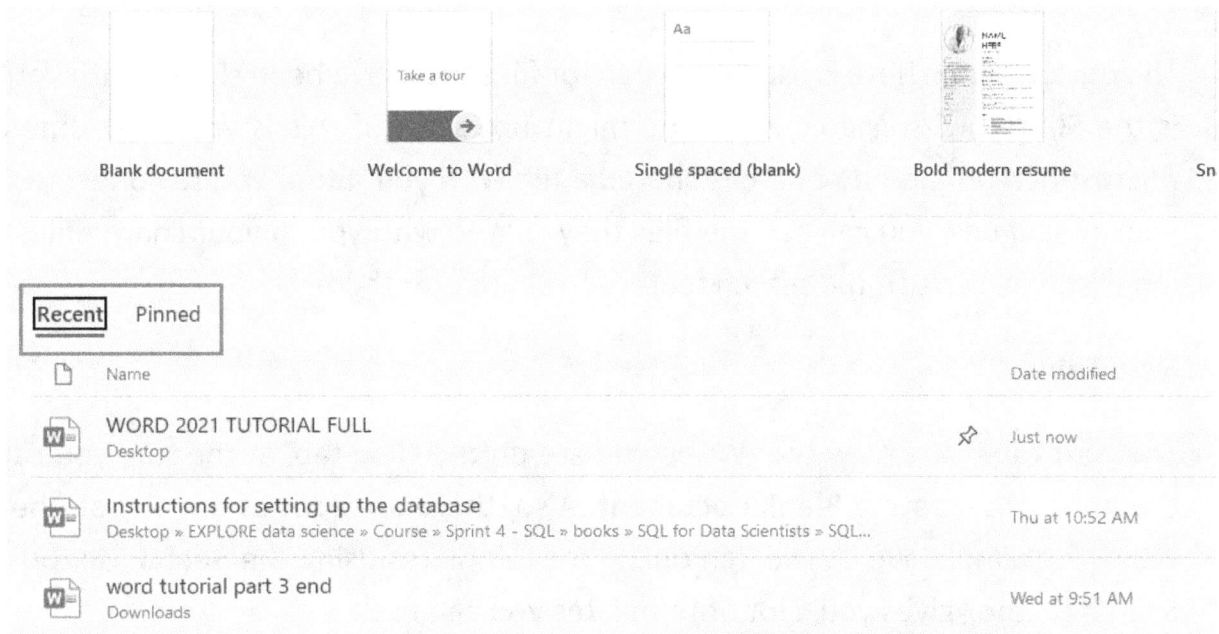

You can see from the picture above that I have some recent files I have been working on. The files are sorted by the newest file first. Then it goes down to the oldest file. You can find the file creation date in the **Date Modified** column.

If you have more documents, you can always click on **More documents**. The more documents feature can be found at the bottom right. The **More Documents** link will show you a longer list of all the files you have been working on.

Besides the **Recent** documents column, you can find the **Pinned** files column. Items you have pinned to the list of Recent documents will appear first, while unpinned documents will appear next in the chronological order they were opened. If you want to find a file later, you can pin it. When you hover over a file, a pin icon will appear. Just click on the pin icon if you want to pin the file.

I can demonstrate this now. Go back to the **Recent** documents column. Your recent files will appear. Then, place your mouse over any file you want to pin. Mousing over one of the files makes a pin icon appear. Click the pin icon to pin your file. Then, go back to the pinned list, and you will find that file among the initial files on the list, if not the first, since this is your first time practicing pinning files.

The other column here is used to search for files that have been shared with you. This is the **Shared with Me** column. You might not see it if this is your first time using Microsoft Word and no one has shared a file with you. But if you're connected with your colleagues, you can see the files they shared with you. If your shared files are a long list, you can use the search feature to search for them.

New Tab

The next tab is the **New tab**. When you are on the New tab, at the top, you can see the option to create a **Blank document**. Also, there are a lot of options on the New tab. For example, we can search online for templates using the **Search** textbox. The Search textbox gives you a lot of templates you can use.

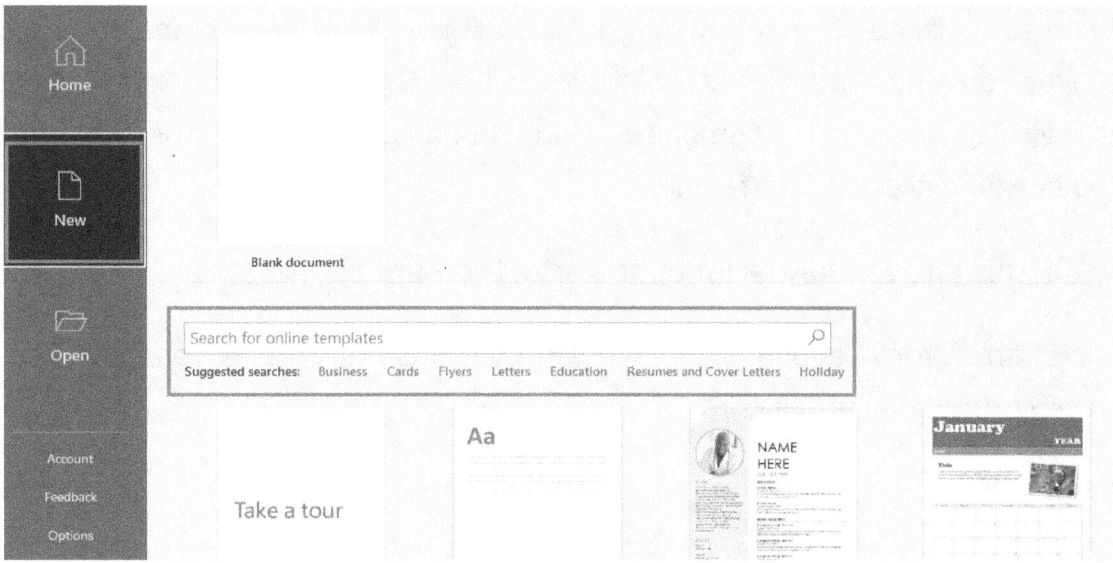

You can also use the Search box to search for particular templates. It will bring up suggested options. If you look at the picture above, you can see that we have some suggested template options like **Business, Cards, Flyers, Letters, education** resumes, and **cover letters**. There is even a suggested template for **holidays**. You should notice that we already have some ready-made templates at the bottom of the Search textbox.

For example, let's take a look at the resume template. Here is the picture of the resume template.

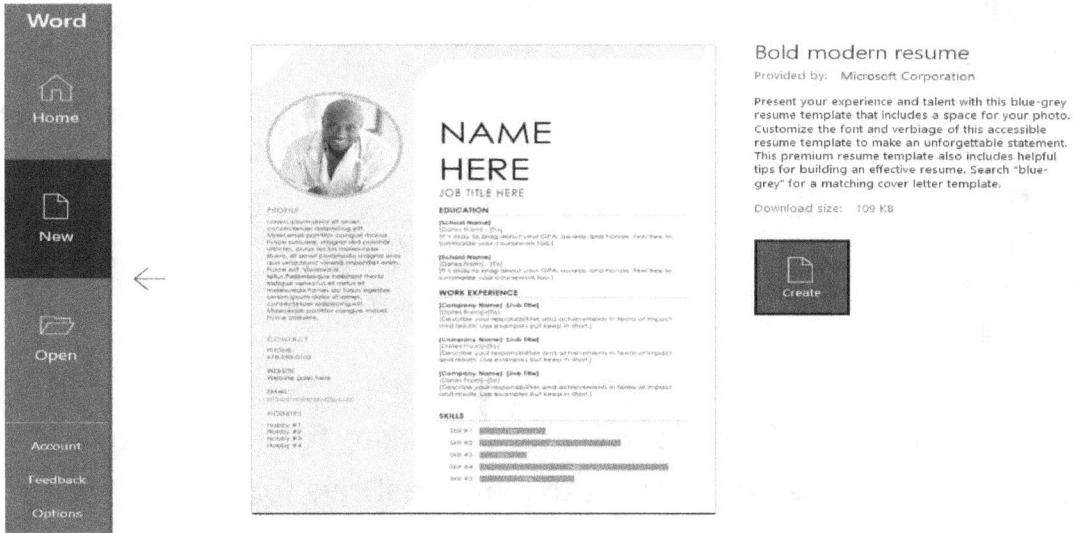

The resume template is ready to use. You just have to fill in your information. Clicking it gives you a nice preview of what it looks like. There is also an excellent description as well. There are many templates. You can navigate through them. If you find one you like, just click on **create** button.

So, on this tab, you have a lot of powerful tools at your fingertips.

Microsoft Word allows you to get various templates online. The link is https://templates.office.com

Open Tab

Then the last tab is the **Open** tab at the bottom. This provides you with a friendly interface where you can find your files. Some of the sections in the Open tab is the **Recent** tab which shows you your recent files, like recent documents and recent folders. It also shows you your pinned files, today's and yesterday's opened files.

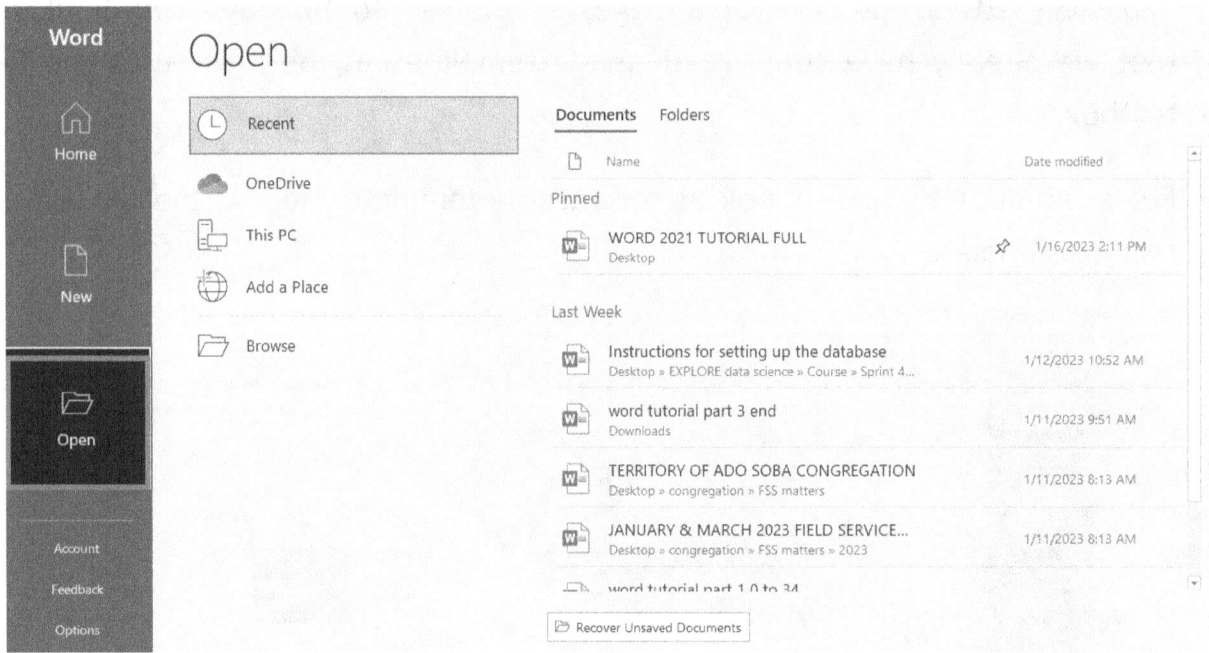

It's a charming way to find whatever you are looking for. In the picture, you can also see that from the Open tab, I can search my **OneDrive** folders and folders on my PC

or even Browse for folders from the computer. So, you have several options to navigate the system looking for your Word document files.

You should try out the **Browse** feature. It will open your computer's folders menu so you can search for files individually.

That's all you can find on the Start Screen. Go ahead and practice what you have learned on your own. Start a blank document. Click on the three tabs - Home, New, and Open tabs. Also, pin some files.

RIBBON

Now that we're familiar with the start screen let's go ahead and start a blank document. Click on the **Home** tab to show you a blank document at the top. Click on the **blank document**. Voila, you are presented with the Microsoft Word interface. If you are familiar with earlier versions of Microsoft Word, you would realize that the ribbon of the latest Microsoft Word is more fascinating.

Now talking about the ribbon. The ribbon is located at the very top of the interface for those new to Microsoft Word. It is formally referred to as the menu in other software. The picture below shows you the ribbon.

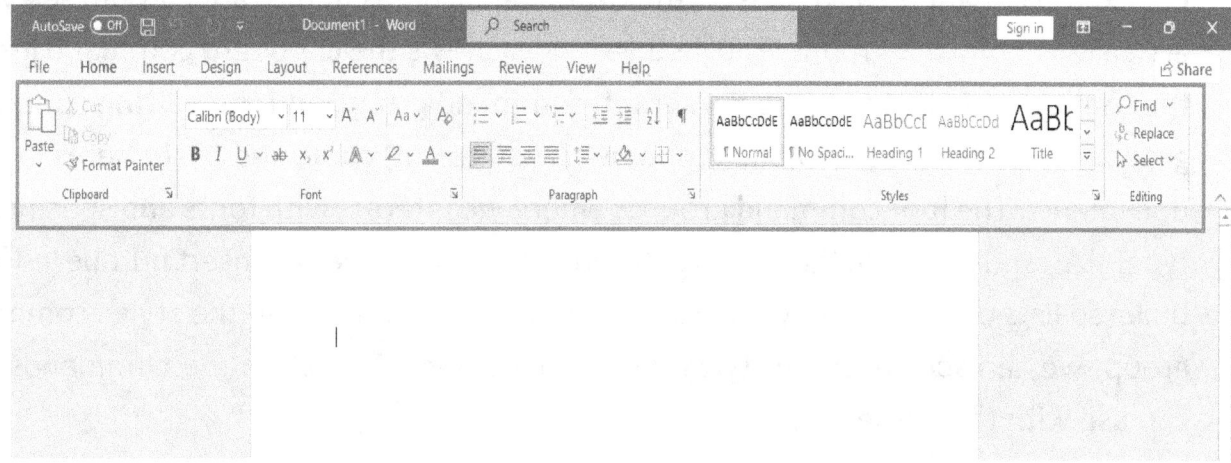

The ribbon is now more visually appealing. Microsoft decided to give it a nice refresh with enormous visual details. Also, you can find things quickly with this ribbon. You will also notice that it has rounded edges towards the outside and shadowy effects when you move over some commands. Take a moment to move your mouse over the commands on the ribbon to see the shadowy effects. Aren't they visually appealing?

Let's start by identifying a few things. Let's see some of its features and how the ribbon works.

First, at the very top of the ribbon are ribbon tabs. We have the **File, Home, Insert, Draw, Design, Layout, Reference, Mailings, Review, View,** and **Help** tabs. You can see them in the picture below.

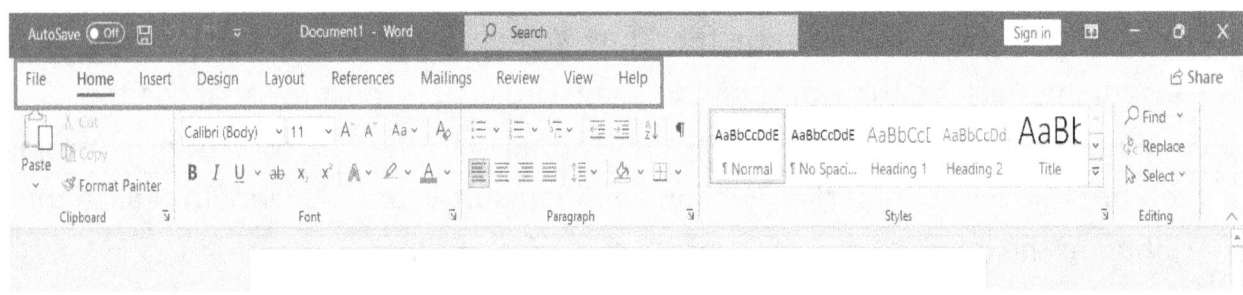

The idea with the interface is that opening one of the ribbon tabs opens up a new set of menus. Let's see how it all works.

For example, right now, we are on the **Home** tab. On this home tab, you can see what are called command groups. The picture below shows the **clipboard** command group, the **font** command group, the **paragraph** command group, and the **editing** command group. The clipboard command group helps you to cut, copy, and paste items in your documents. The font command group is where we interact with fonts and specify font type, size, and color. On the paragraph command group, we can insert numbered lists, bulleted lists or even specify the alignment of our documents. In the styles command group, we can specify some styles for the document. These are the commands you can use with the home tab.

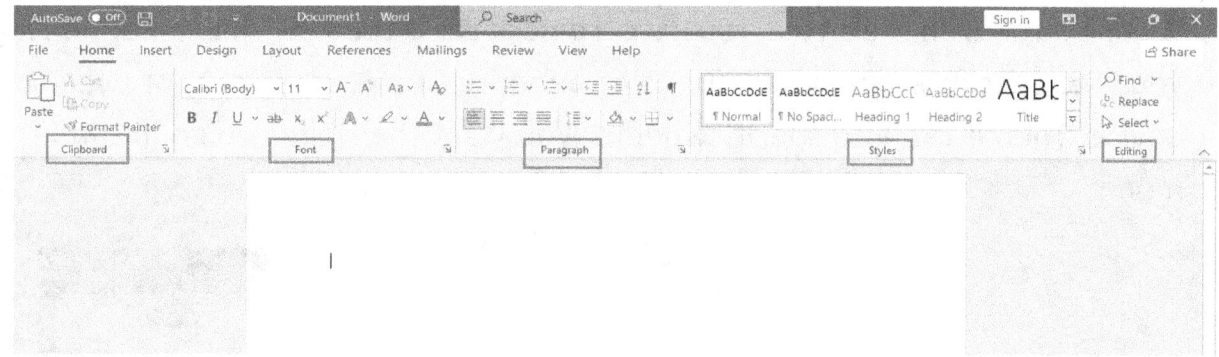

Let's try out another tab. This time let's click on the **Insert** tab. As you can see after clicking it, the insert tab has its command groups, and each command group has its commands. We interact with these commands to do things on our documents.

Another function you should be aware of is that you can scroll through the tabs. Just place your mouse between any two tabs. Then move the mouse between the tabs while the left key is down. It gives you the ability to scroll instantly across the tabs.

Hiding/Unhiding Ribbon

I want to bring your attention to another feature on the ribbon. For example, you don't want to simultaneously see all the ribbon commands and their features. You can make use of the **ribbon display options** feature. You can find it at the top right, just below the ribbon at the right. It is like a tiny dropdown arrow. When you click on the arrow, it brings up the display options for your ribbon.

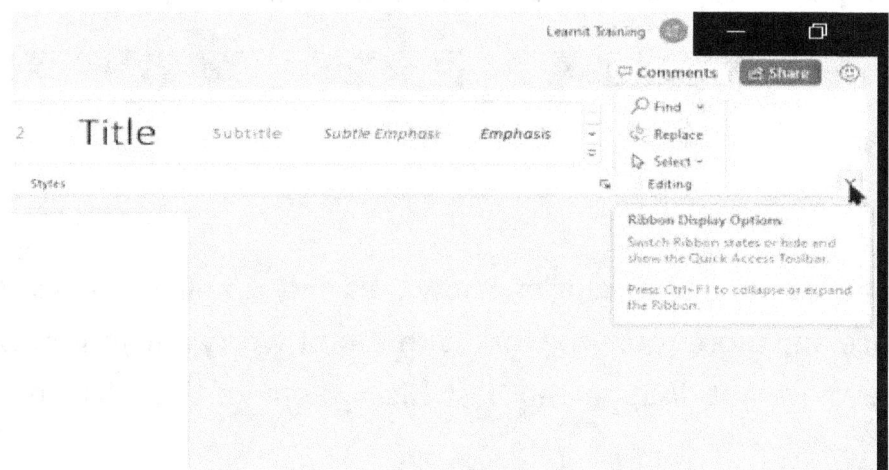

When you click on the arrow, you have a **quick access toolbar**. The first option it gives you is to specify whether you are using a mouse or a touchscreen, or even a touch device. Then it can also specify whether you want the ribbon to go into full-screen mode.

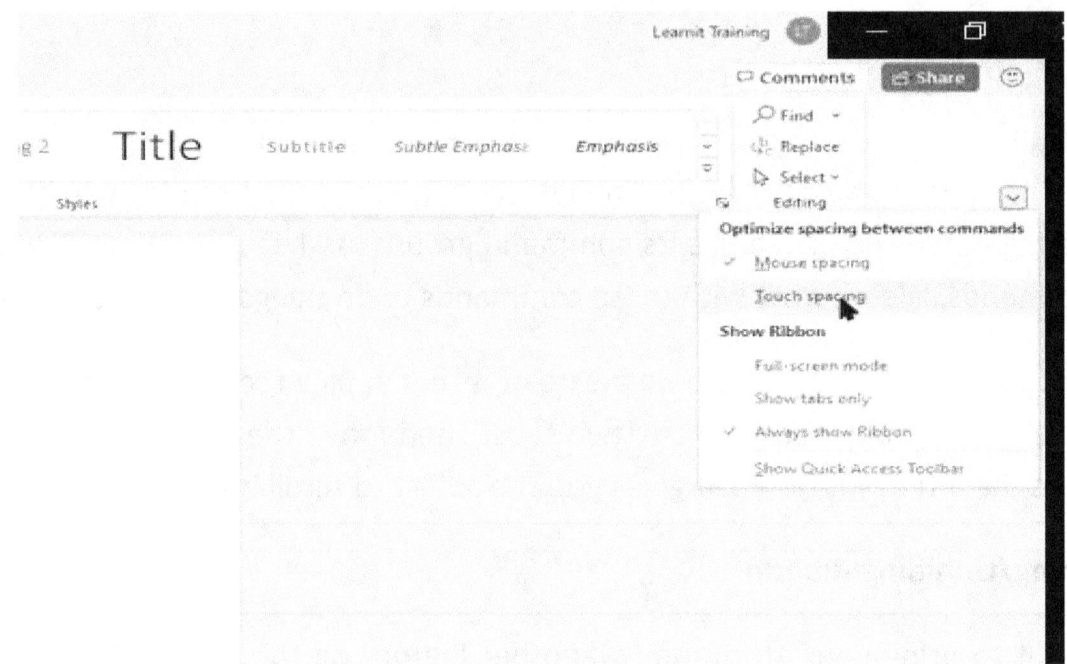

When you mouse over a command, it shows you what it does. That's one great thing about Microsoft products. On **Show tabs only,** you will maximize the window and hide the ribbon. It also hides the quick access toolbar. This simplifies the ribbon and makes you see only the tabs. Try it and see what happens.

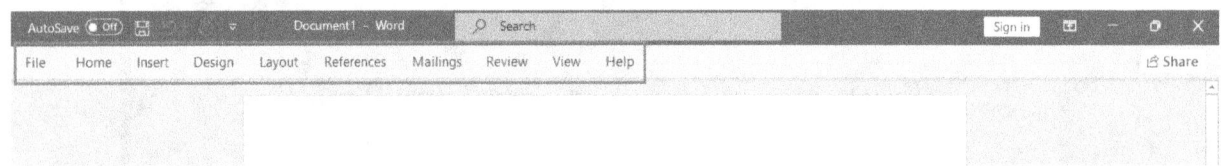

You must have seen that clicking on **Show tabs only** simplifies things. It gives you more visual space and more room to work with. Don't worry; all your ribbon tabs are still there. They have not disappeared. Just click on one of the tabs, and it gets revealed again.

Another option you can specify is to **Always show the ribbon**. This way, it pins the ribbon to the tabs and gets shown all the time. It's really up to you to choose your options based on your goals.

Quick Access Toolbar

Another feature in the Word software is the quick access toolbar. You can enable the **Quick Access Toolbar** by right-clicking any command, and the menu for it comes up. You then select the "**Quick Access Toolbar.**" That command gets added to the Quick Access Toolbar.

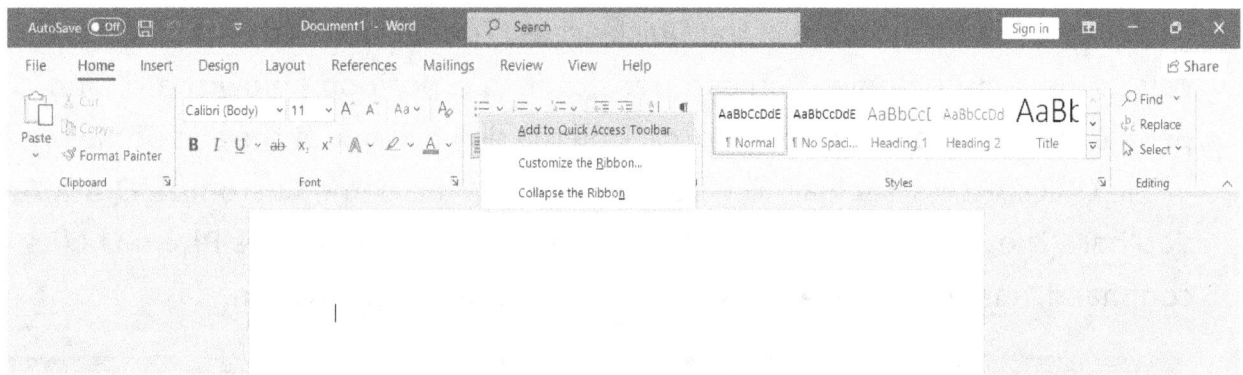

The Quick Access Toolbar is a way to give us quick access to some of the commands that we use in Microsoft Word. The Quick Access Toolbar is found above the tabs.

I will go ahead and customize the Quick Access Toolbar. There are many things I like frequently using on Microsoft Word, so I will choose those by hovering over the command, right-clicking, and selecting **Add to the Quick Access Toolbar.** This is a picture to show the commands I have added.

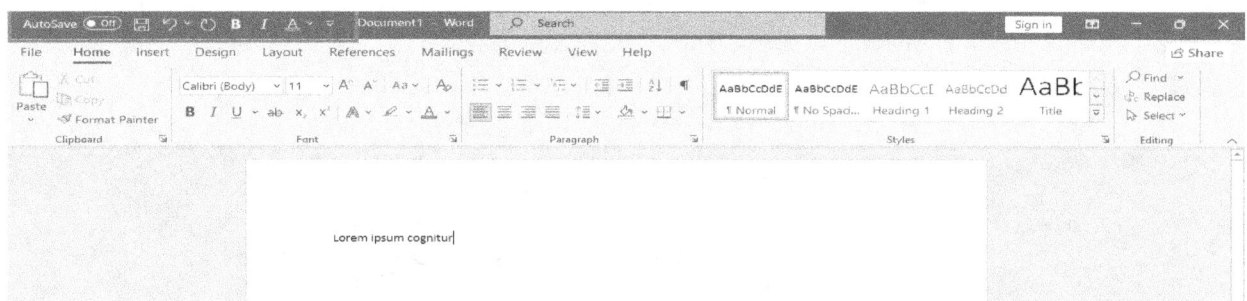

You can see that the Quick Access Toolbar contains the **Autosave** command, **undo** command, **bold, Italics,** and **Font** color commands.

Now with these tools in my Quick Access Toolbar, even if I am on any command tab, I can quickly access them without going back to the tab that contains these commands.

You can also remove items added to your Quick Access Toolbar. To remove an item or command, just right-click on it and choose the button that says **Remove from Quick Access Toolbar.**

If you don't like the position of the Quick Access Toolbar above the ribbon, as I showed you in the picture above, you can transfer it to a position below the ribbon. Some people prefer it that way. To do so, click on the down arrow at the end of the last item in the Quick Access Toolbar. The down arrow has the name **Customize Quick Access Toolbar.** The last command in that menu is **Show below the Ribbon.** Click that command, and the Quick Access Toolbar will go below the ribbon.

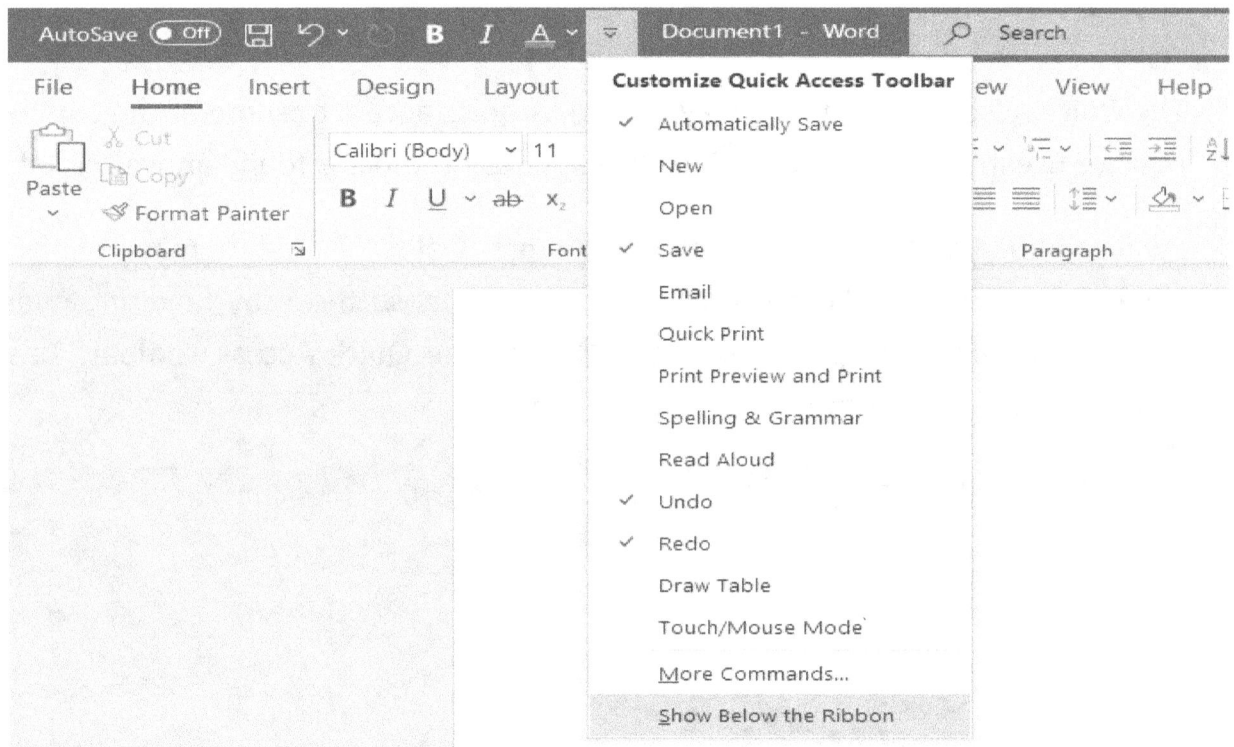

You can see it is now below the ribbon.

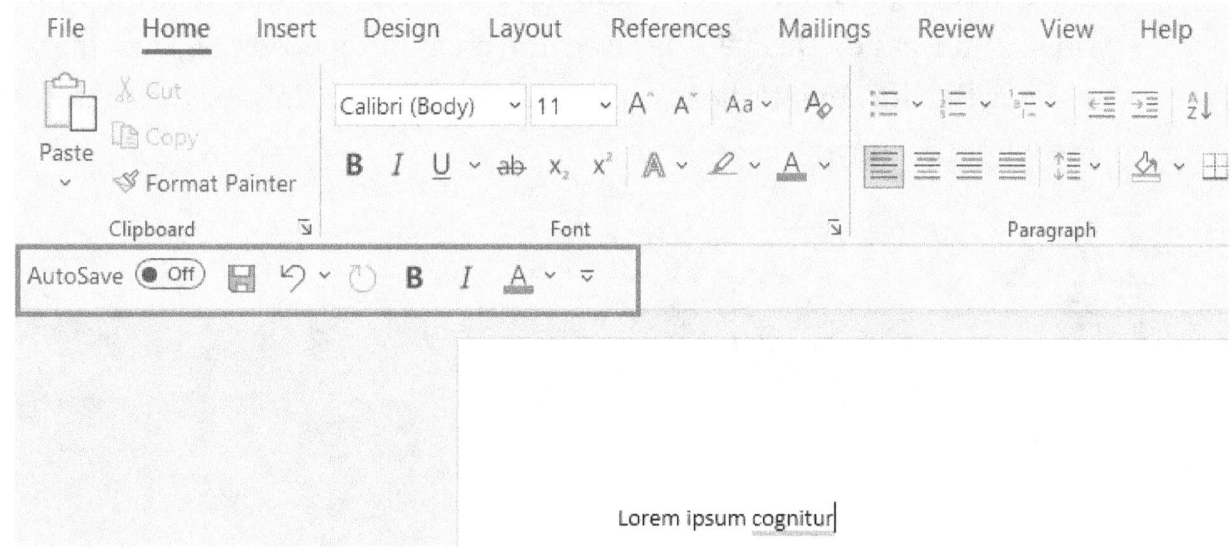

It's really up to you what position to put the Quick Access Toolbar in.

You are now more comfortable and familiar with Microsoft Word at this stage. Go ahead and try out all the features shown to you. Make sure you practice them. Try practicing adding some commands to the Quick Access Toolbar. Practicing these tasks will make you more familiar with Microsoft Word.

NAVIGATION PANE

Now I want to show you something we can do with the **navigation pane**. But first, let us go to the **View** tab. From the View tab, we can see the **Show** command groups. I want you to concentrate on three commands in this command group.

1. **Ruler**: The ruler will help us to establish tab stops. It adjusts the margins and indents of a document. It also sets measurements for the columns and other layout elements. Additionally, you can use the ruler to create and edit tables in the document.

2. **Grid lines**: Gridlines help create precise layouts in a document. They can also be used to align tables. You can also use them as a guide when drawing shapes.
3. **Navigation pane**: This can be used for creating and editing bookmarks and viewing the document's headers and sections. It is mainly used as a preview of the whole document.

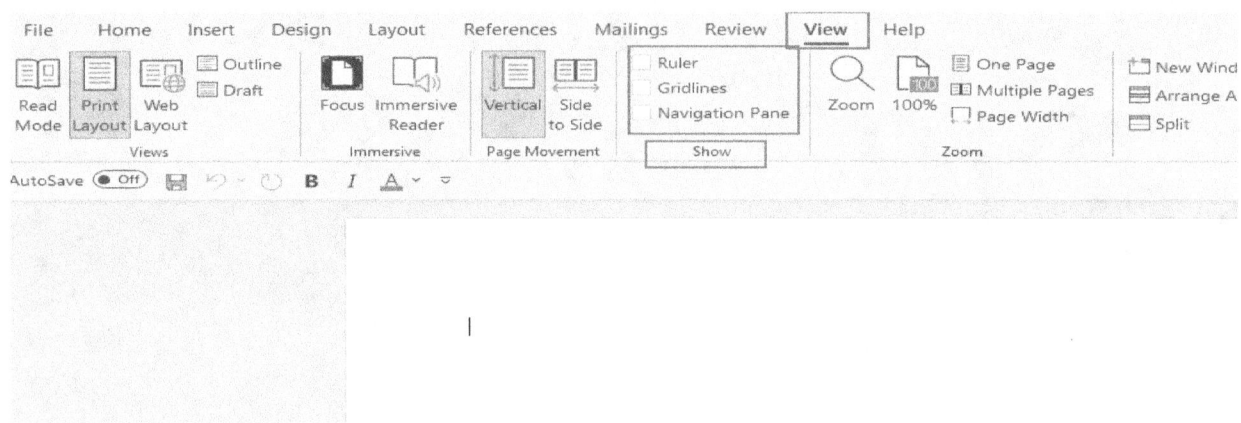

So, let me go ahead and turn on the ruler and gridlines.

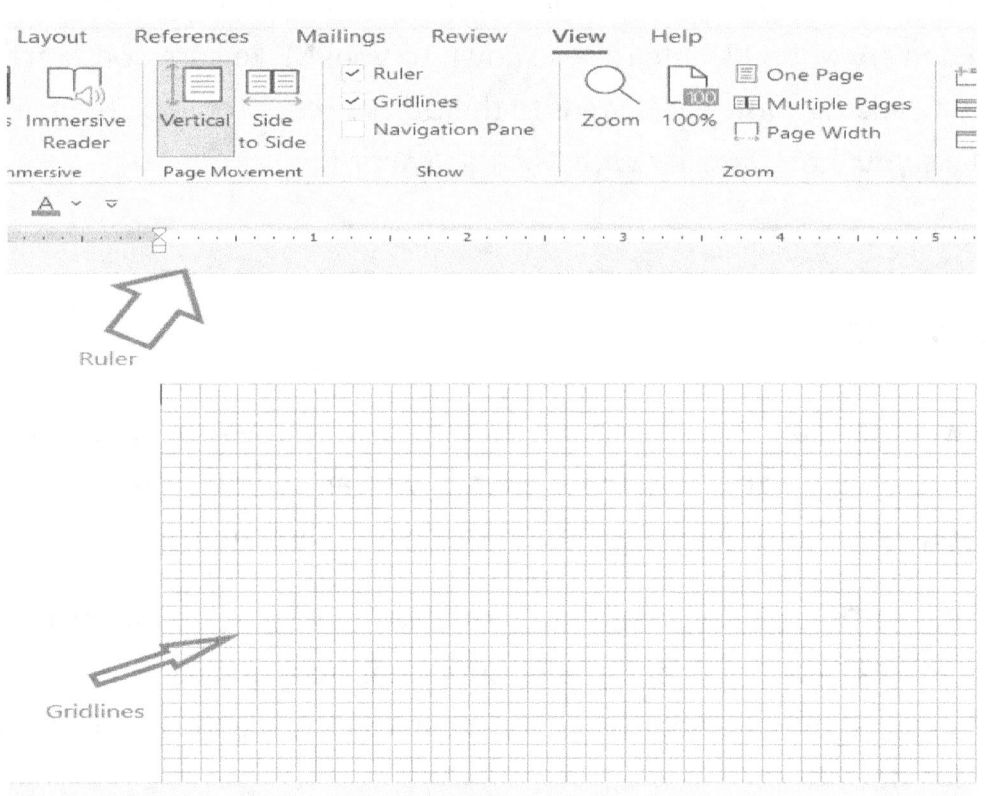

Then let's turn on the navigation pane. The navigation pane opens up on the left. You can search the navigation pane. You can take a look at **headings, pages,** and **results**. The headings show any headings in your document, while the pages tab shows all the pages in the document. My document has only one page, so it shows only one page. The results tab helps you to search for anything in your document. Microsoft Word will highlight any match found in the document based on whatever you search. The highlight will be in yellow. In the picture below, I searched for the word "**tabs**" in the document, and you can see them highlighted. The results are shown at the left so you can quickly navigate to a match.

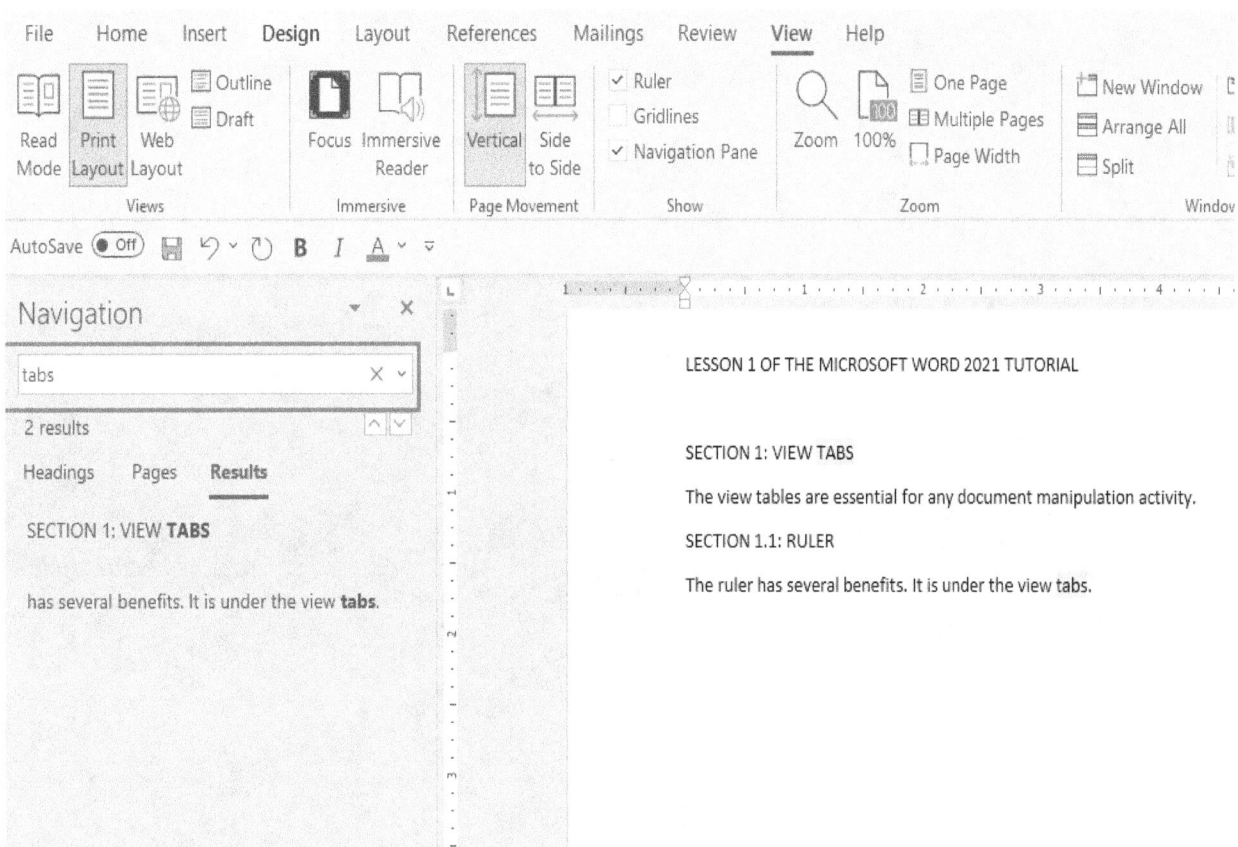

It's not only keywords that are searchable. You can also search for phrases or even sentences. In the picture below, you can see how the phrase I searched for is highlighted instantly.

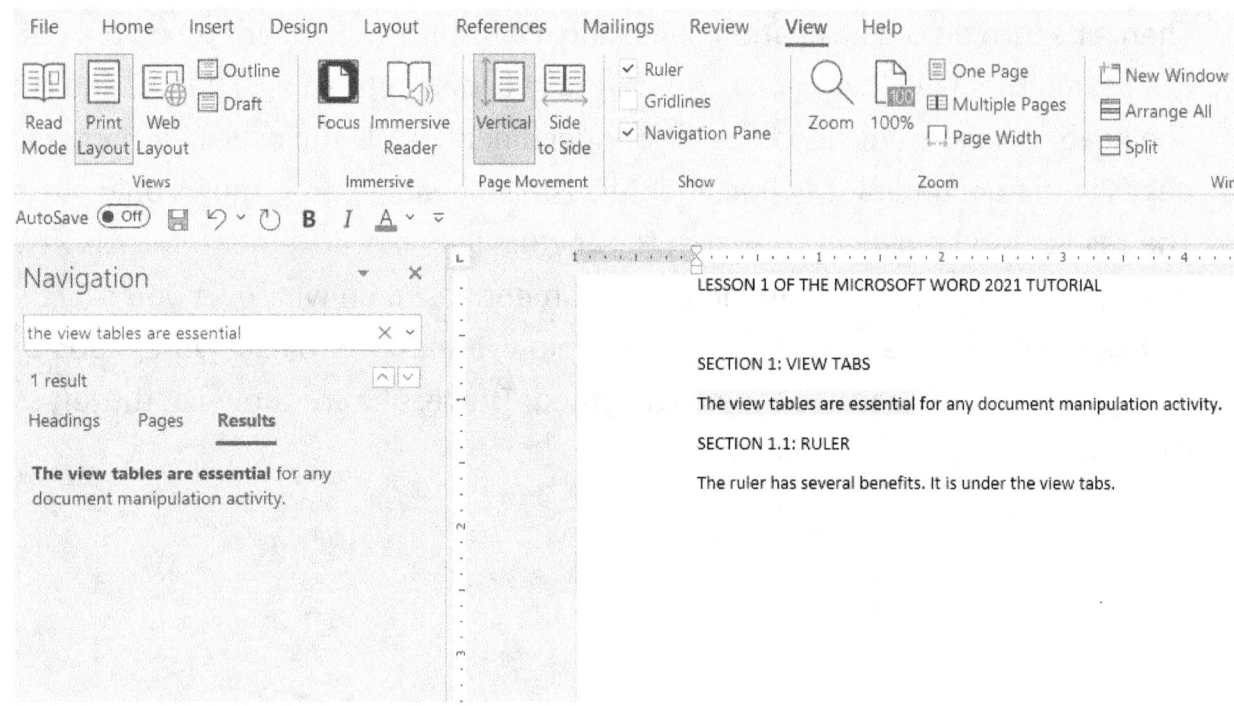

LESSON 1 OF THE MICROSOFT WORD 2021 TUTORIAL

SECTION 1: VIEW TABS

The view tables are essential for any document manipulation activity.

SECTION 1.1: RULER

The ruler has several benefits. It is under the view tabs.

PART TWO FORMATTING TEXT AND PARAGRAPH LAYOUTS

Formatting text and creating concise paragraph layouts give your documents an appealing look. In this chapter, we will discuss these subjects along with ways to create lists.

FORMATTING TEXT

To format text, we need to have text on the document. So, I created some text for this section. Formatting makes information more accessible and visually appealing to the reader. In this section, I will show you some formatting you can carry out on your document in Microsoft Word.

For formatting text, we are talking about features in the **Font** group under the **Home** tab.

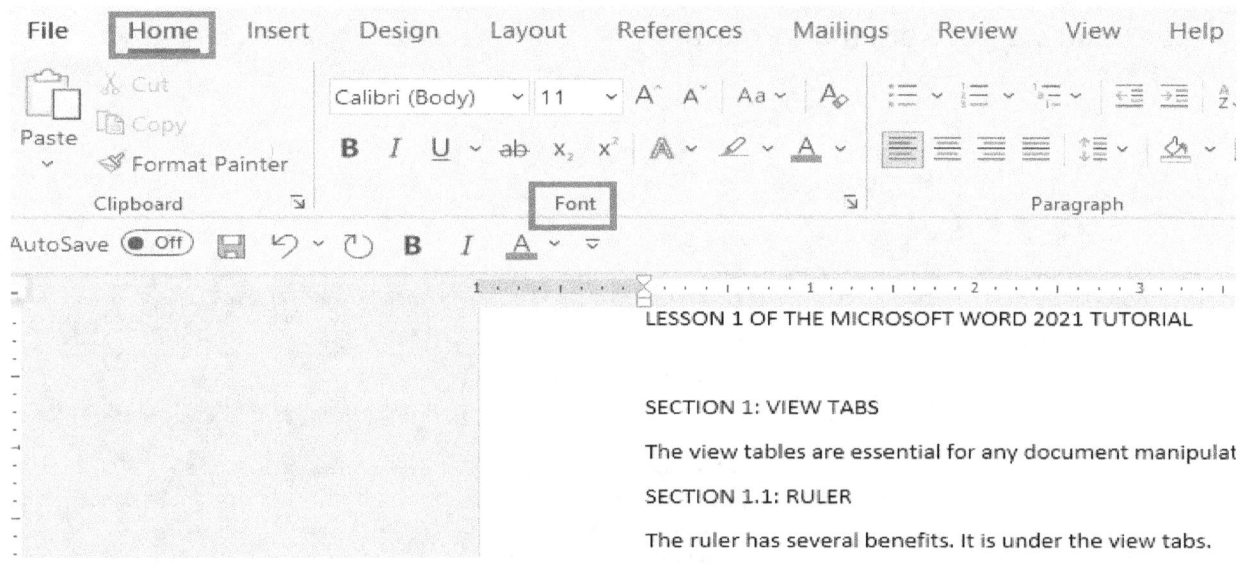

Let's practice some of the features you can find in this group.

To begin, select some text in any document. Go to the font group. You will find various features like **Font size, Bold, Font,** etc. We'll try out these. I selected the first text in my document with "**LESSON 1 OF THE MICROSOFT WORD TUTORIAL**." Once it is selected, I went to the **font** command groups and choose "**Bold**." Then I changed the font size to 20. Then I underlined it by clicking **Underline.** The picture below shows the result of all of these actions.

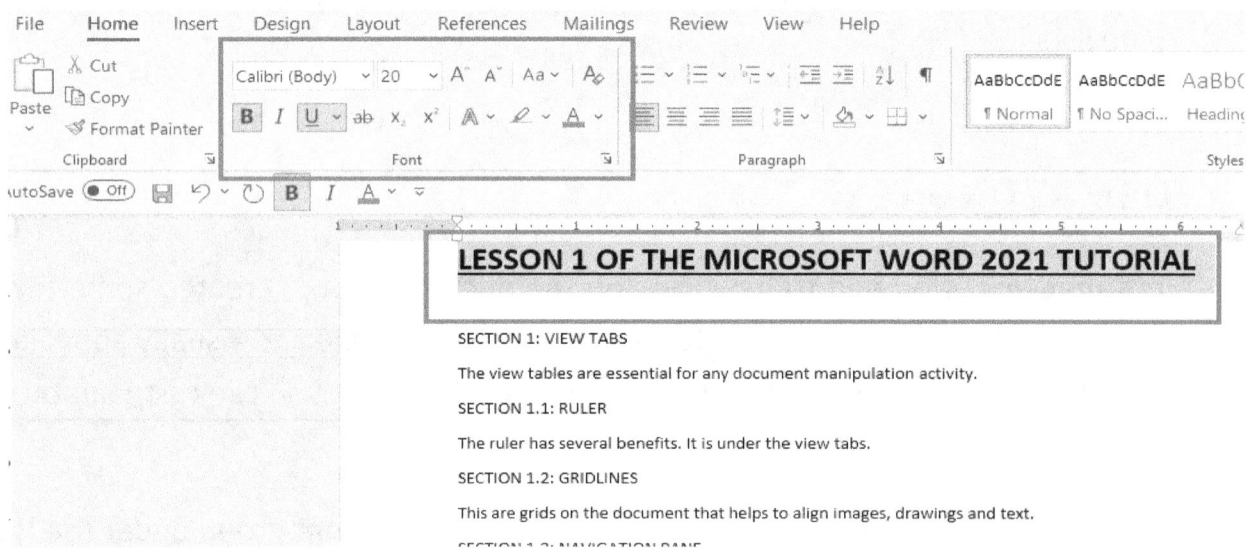

I will do some more formatting. I will click on **italics** and change the **font color** to red. See what we get from the formatting.

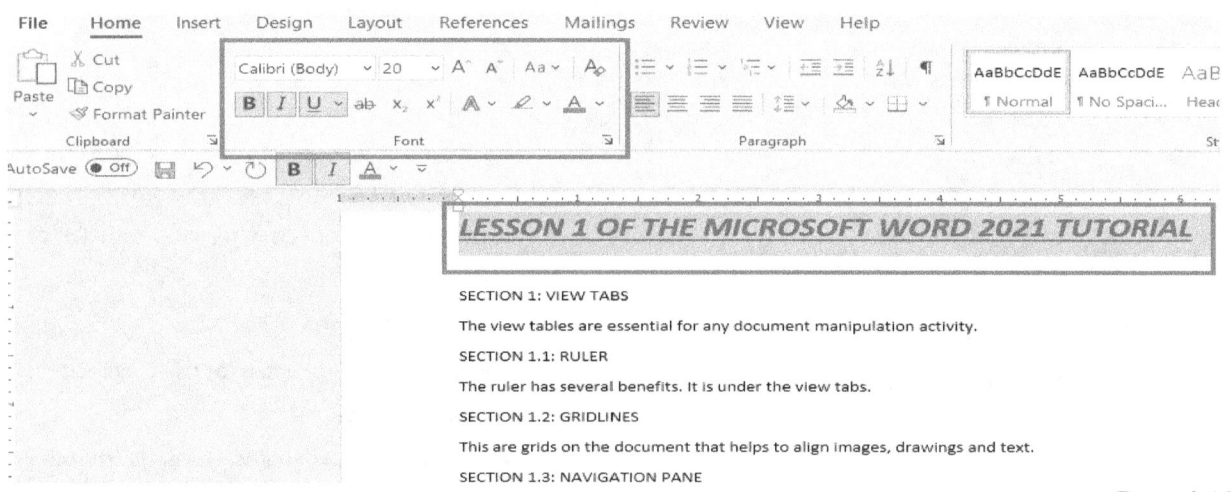

While choosing the different commands, did you notice that when your mouse was over the command, a text box appeared that showed you the name of the command and its shortcut? Try it again to see it. You will notice that the shortcut for **bold** is **CTRL+B** and that for **underline** is **CTRL+U**. You can easily apply these commands to your document when you memorize the shortcuts.

This is something I also want you to try out. If you have a text you want to format, click on those text three times. You will find that a mini command tool will appear like the picture below.

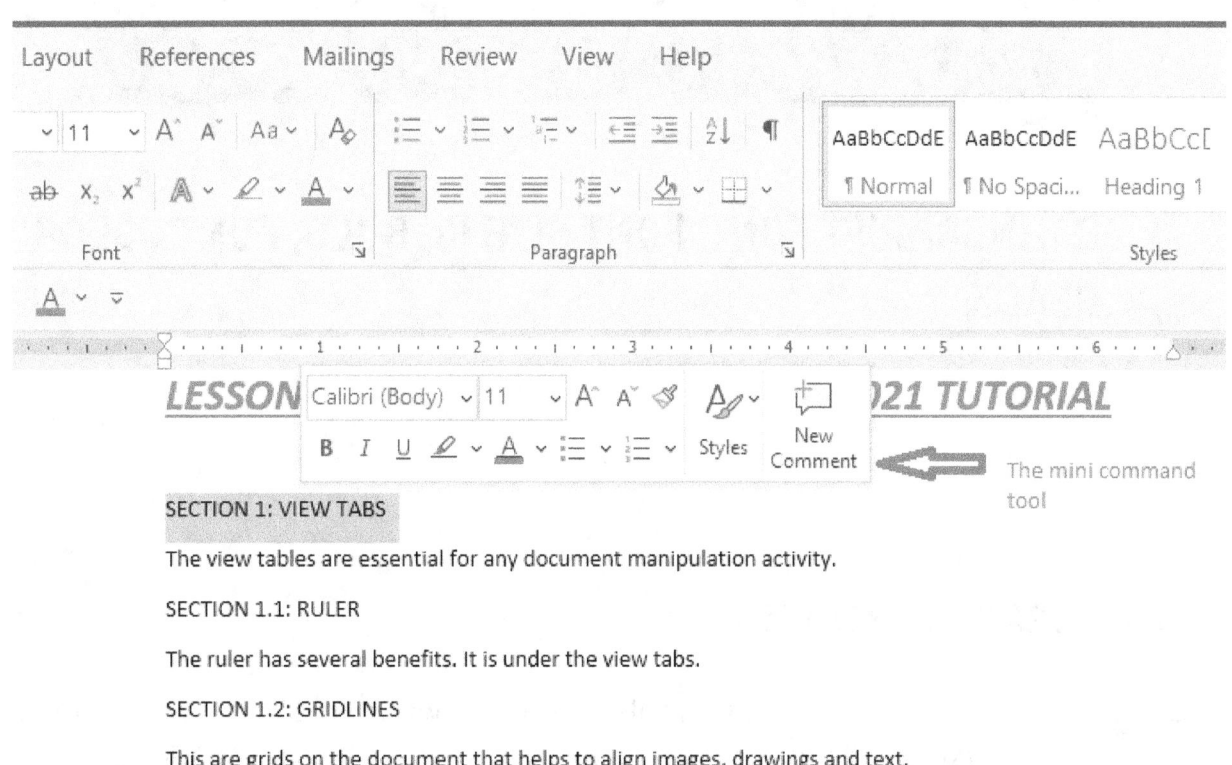

The mini-command tool contains the basic formatting commands you can use on your documents. It is another shortcut for making formatting faster.

In the picture below, there are four lines of formatting applied. Each line states what formatting you should practice. Can you practice it to reproduce the formatting in the picture?

Let's give it a try.

CALIBRI FONT, FONT SIZE 12, BOLD, ITALICS AND FONT COLOR BLUE

ALGERIAN FONT, FONT SIZE 14, UNDERLINE, AND FONT COLOR RED

ARIAL BLACK FONT, FONT SIZE 16, ITALICS, FONT COLOR YELLOW AND TEXT HIGHTLIGHT COLOR BLUE

BAHNSCHRIFT FONT, FONT SIZE 18, BOLD, FONT COLOR BLACK

PARAGRAPH LAYOUTS

Before we dive deep into paragraph layouts, I want to show you some of the objectives we left out earlier. That is, how to copy and paste content. I have some content in another document, say on a notepad, and I want to bring it into this document. I need to copy that content. Do you remember the famous command for copying content? Select the content range and click **CTRL+C**. That's famous on every Microsoft software.

Now, how do we paste this content into our document? You go to the clipboard command groups and select the Paste command.

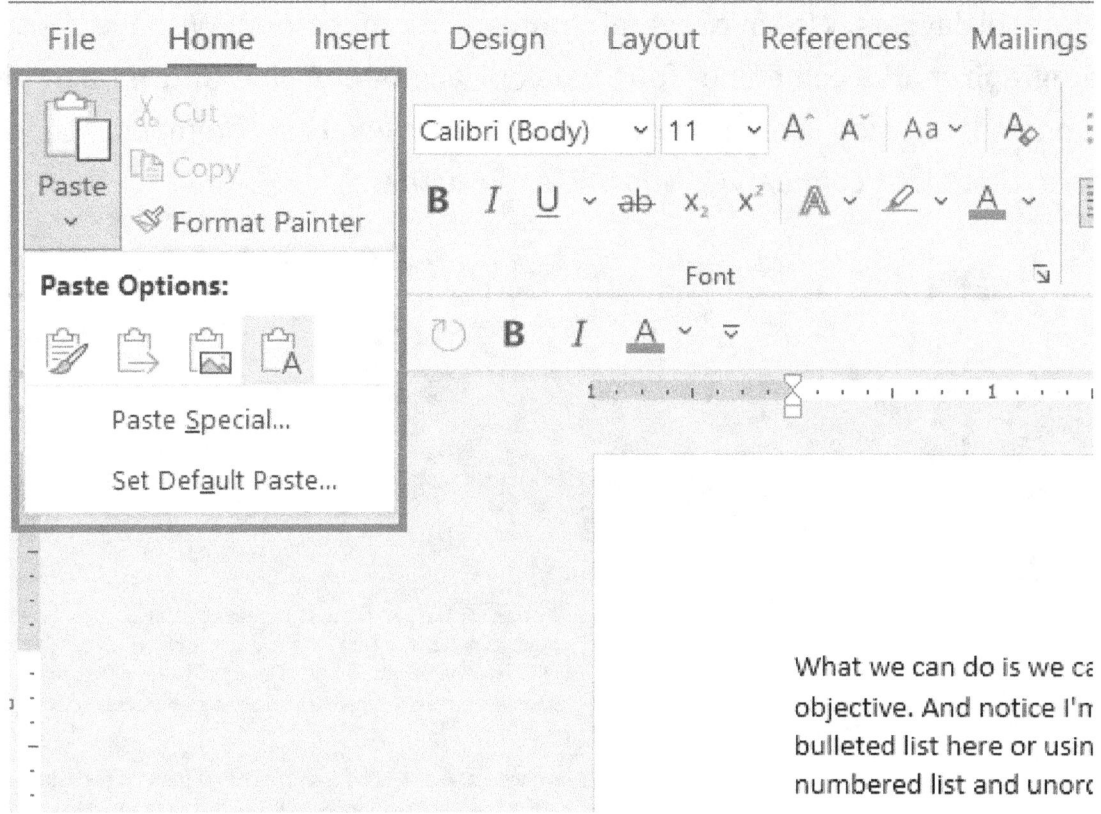

From the picture above, you can see that we have four paste options:

1. **Keep source formatting**: This pastes the content with the formatting from the source document.
2. **Merge formatting**: This combines the formatting from the source document with that of our present document.
3. **Picture**: If an image is in the source document, it will paste into the new document.
4. **Keep text only**: Only text without pictures or formatting will be pasted into the new document.

Alternatively, you can use **CTRL + V** to directly paste a copied content.

Now that we know how to copy and paste contents, let's dive deep into paragraph layouts. We need to be in the home tab and the paragraph command group for the paragraph layouts. We have several commands in that group. We have the **show/hide paragraph marks** command, four types of **alignment**, **line and paragraph spacing** command, **bulleted list, numbered list**, and **multilevel list** commands. There are a lot more. Go to that command group and explore them.

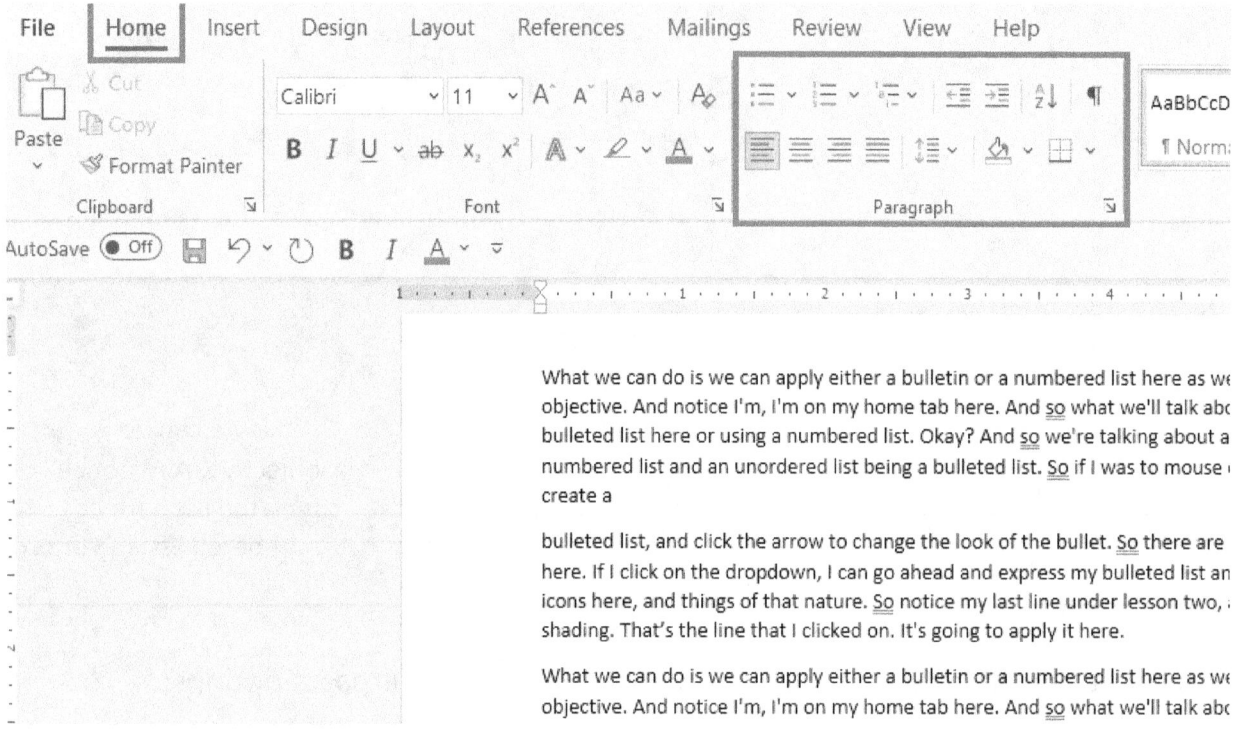

Alignment

The alignment commands will help you arrange the edge of your paragraph in a certain way. We have four types of alignment in Microsoft Word. They are **Align Left**, **Center**, **Align Right**, and **Justify**.

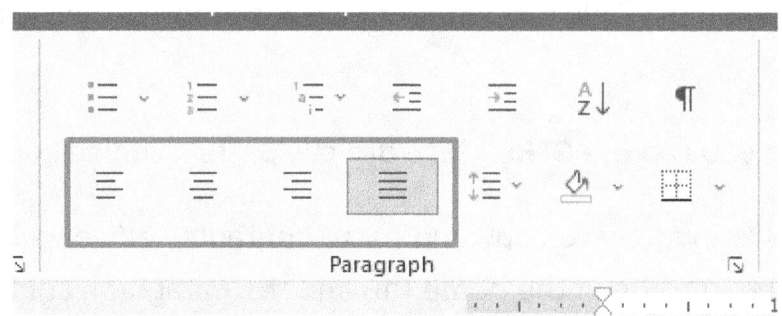

To use these commands, you must have selected/highlighted the paragraph(s). Then, choose one of the commands depending on your style of writing.

The images below describe the four types of alignment.

When you **align left**, you have a paragraph that looks this way. The alignment commands will help you arrange the edge of your paragraph in a certain way. We have four types of alignment in Microsoft Word. They are Align Left, Center, Align Right, and Justify. To use these commands, you must have selected/highlighted the paragraph(s). Then, choose one of the commands depending on your style of writing.

When your alignment is **center**, you have a paragraph that looks this way. The alignment commands will help you arrange the edge of your paragraph in a certain way. We have four types of alignment in Microsoft Word. They are Align Left, Center, Align Right, and Justify. To use these commands, you must have selected/highlighted the paragraph(s). Then, choose one of the commands depending on your style of writing.

When you **align right**, you have a paragraph that looks this way. The alignment commands will help you arrange the edge of your paragraph in a certain way. We have four types of alignment in Microsoft Word. They are Align Left, Center, Align Right, and Justify. To use these commands, you must have selected/highlighted the paragraph(s). Then, choose one of the commands depending on your style of writing.

When your alignment is **justify**, you have a paragraph that looks this way. The alignment commands will help you arrange the edge of your paragraph in a certain way. We have four types of alignment in Microsoft Word. They are Align Left, Center, Align Right, and Justify. To use these commands, you must have selected/highlighted the paragraph(s). Then, choose one of the commands depending on your style of writing.

Line and Paragraph Spacing

Let's take one of the options, the **line and paragraph spacing**. Notice how the spacing between lines becomes wider when I chose 2.5 spacing between lines.

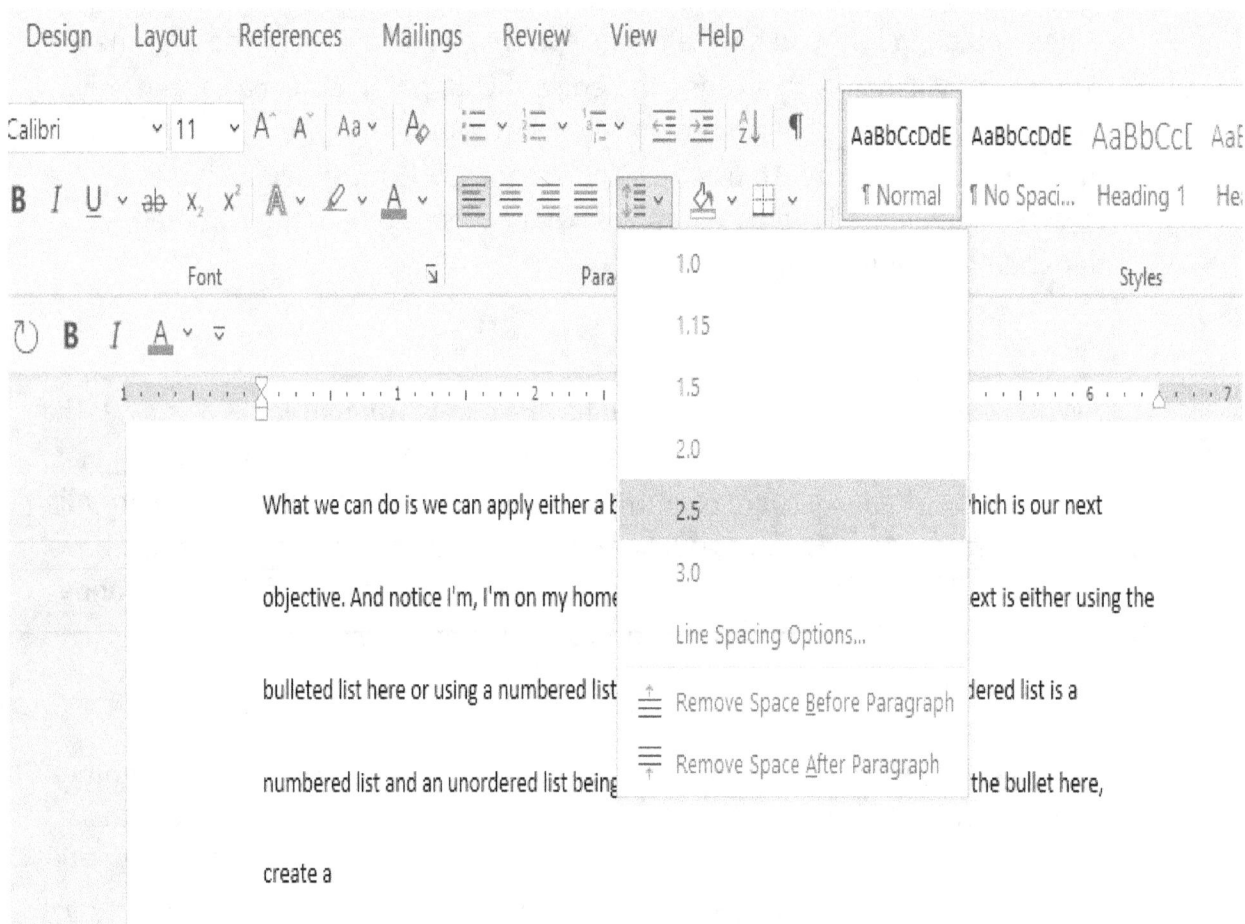

You can get more line spacing features by choosing the **Line spacing options**, as seen in the picture above. When you click on that option, you get a new dialog box that gives you all the line spacing features you can apply to a document.

The first tab to open is the **indent and spacing** tab. You can set fine-grained controls for **alignment, outline level**, and **spacing**. Play around with these controls on a document to see how they work. Follow along with the preview at the bottom to see how everything will play out in the document.

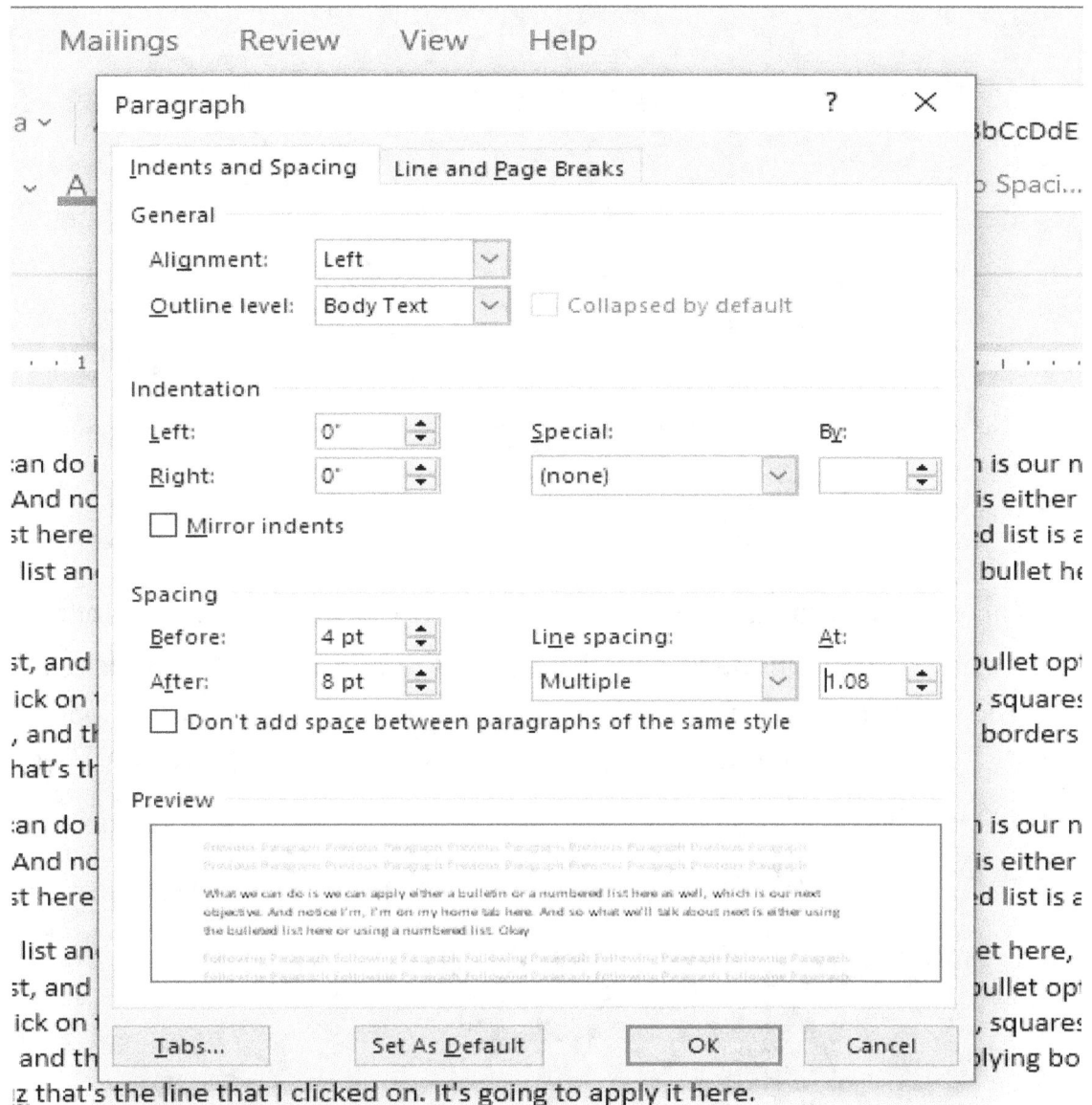

We need to go to the **Design** tab to change the spacing for the whole document, not just the line or paragraph level. We need to go to the **Document Formatting** command group and choose **Paragraph Spacing**. When you click on the dropdown menu on the paragraph spacing, it shows you the different templates for spacing your document. For example, if we choose the **Tight** paragraph spacing, we can see that the spacing before the paragraph is 0 pt, the spacing after the paragraph is 6 pt, and the line spacing for the document will be 1.15.

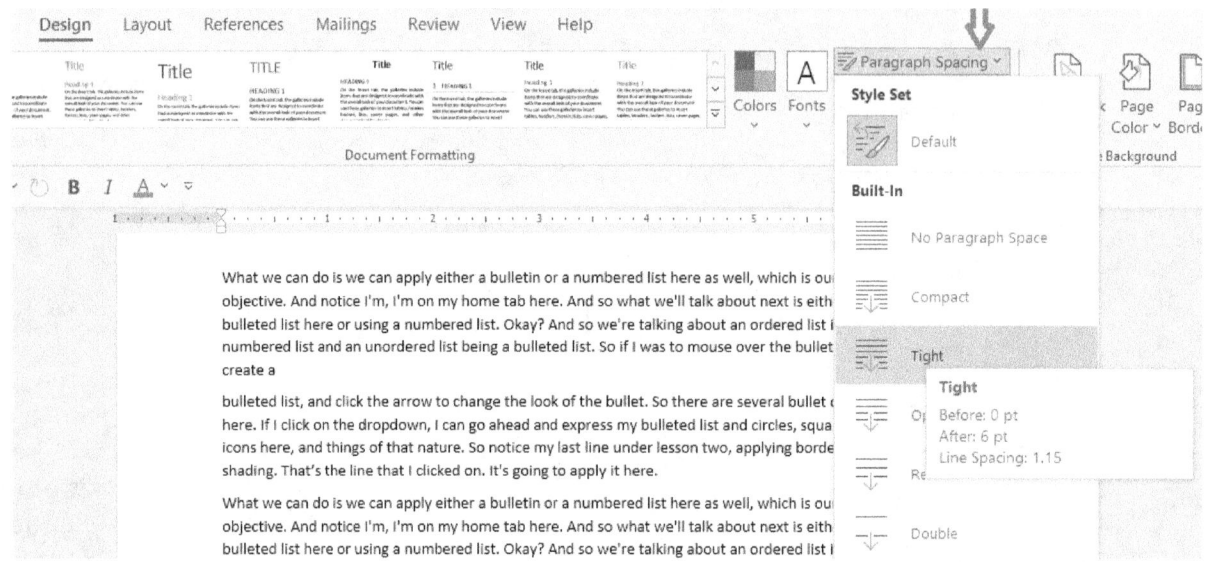

You can specify paragraph spacing by going to the bottom of the **Style Set** in the paragraph spacing command and clicking on **Custom Paragraph Spacing.** You get a whole lot more options to specify. You can set the custom paragraph spacing only for this document or for any new document produced in Microsoft Word software licensed to you.

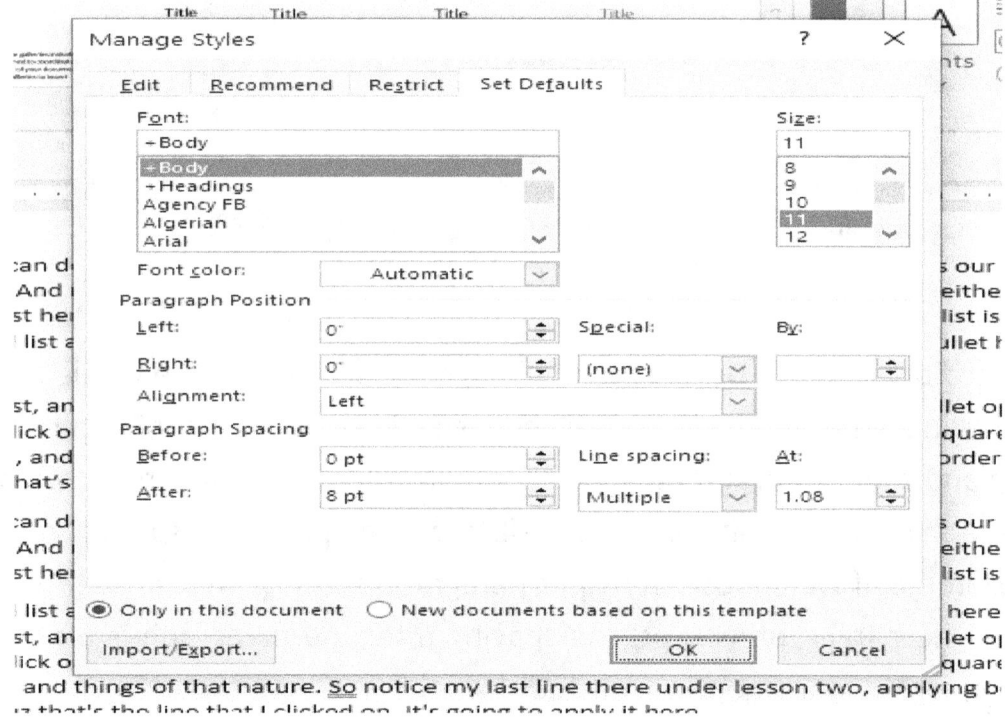

So go ahead and practice these commands for paragraph layouts. Try to get a feel for how they work because you will use them a lot in styling the documents in your paragraph.

CREATING LISTS

Imagine in your document you have objectives you want to define. Or you want to list out some specific items in the document. We can make use of a **numbered** or **bulleted** list. You can find these among the **paragraph** command groups in the **Home** tab.

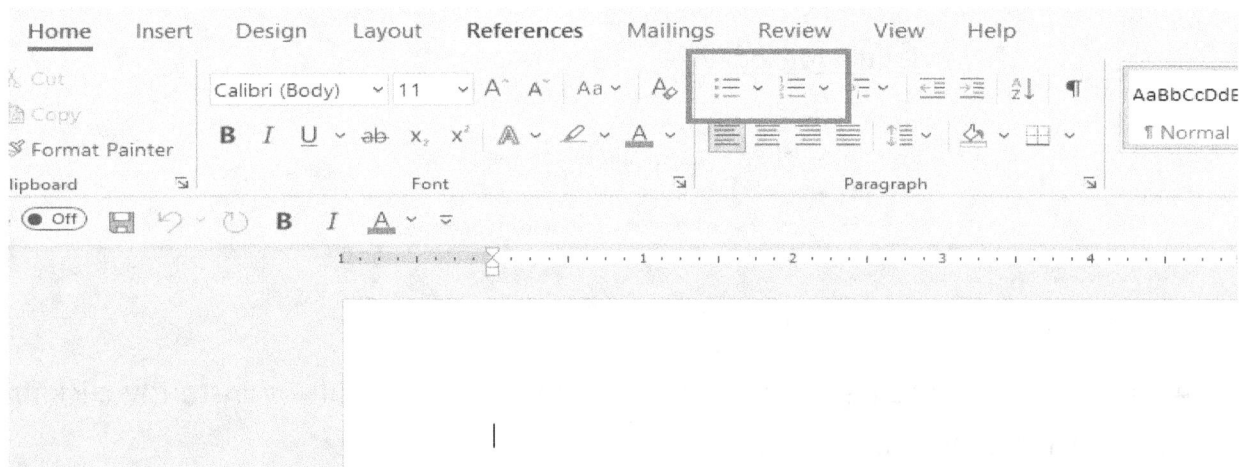

When you need an ordered list, you use a numbered list, but when you need an unordered list, you use a bulleted list.

Let's explore creating a bulleted list.

You first select the content on the document you want to create as a bulleted list. Then, you can choose various types of the bulleted list by clicking the dropdown beside the bulleted list command. You will find the different types of bullets in the bulleted list, like **circles, squares, transparent circles**, etc. They are all in the bullet library. A preview comes with each type of bullet you select. The picture below shows this.

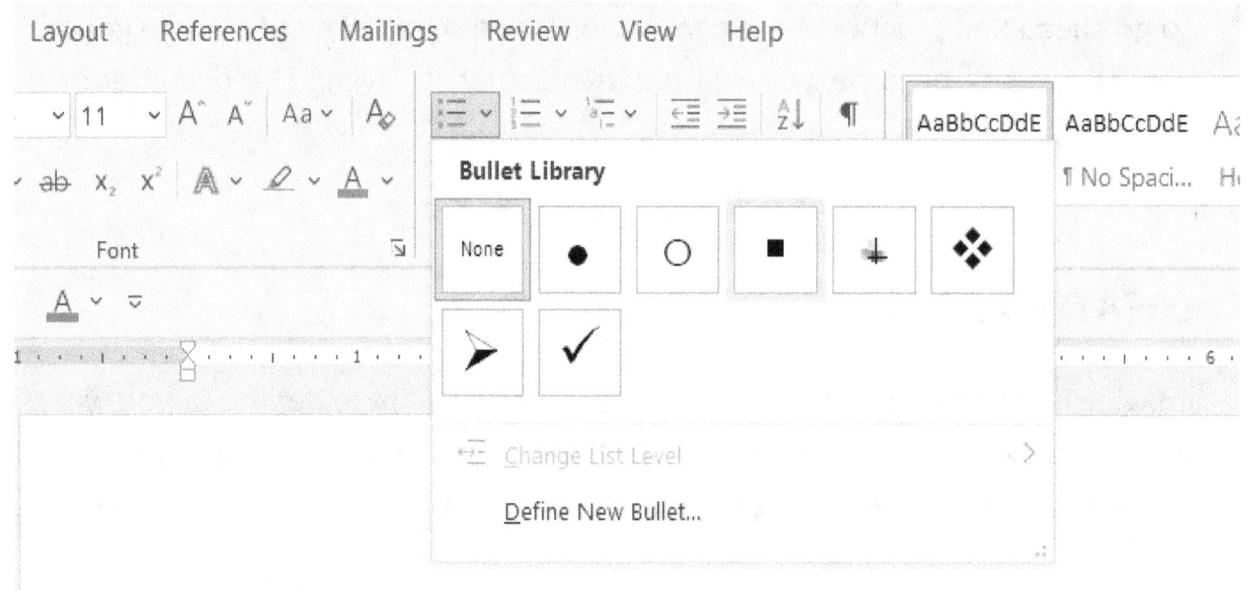

Also, you can define new bullets or just choose the default by instantly clicking the bulleted list command.

From the picture above, you can see that all the objectives in the document are aligned with the bullets beside them.

Now, let's try using a numbered list. As I told you, you use a numbered list when your content is ordered.

To use a numbered list, select the content you want to number. Then click on the dropdown arrow beside the **Numbering** command. A series of options in the **Numbering library** appears. Choose the option in the library you want while checking the preview. In the picture below, I used the **Number alignment: Left**" option. You can see how the numbered list appears in the preview below the image.

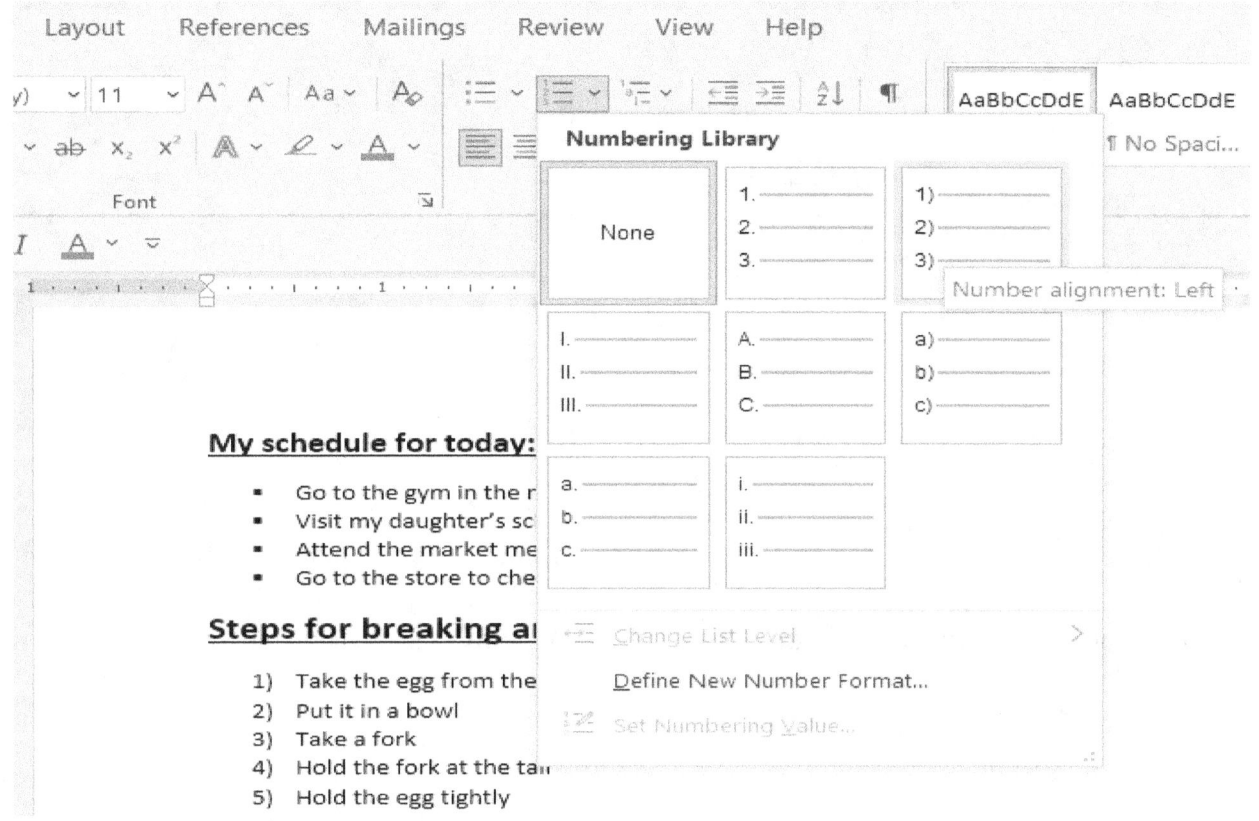

You have the option to define a new number format. Also, you can use the default by clicking on the Numbering command.

After creating a bulleted or numbered list, you can automatically insert new elements at the end of the list. To do so, just go to the last item in the list and click the Enter key. A new item is inserted into the list immediately. If you want to leave the list, just click on Enter twice.

You can change the symbol you used for a numbered or bulleted list if you don't like it. All you need to do is select the list and then go to the **bullet** or **numbering library**. From the library, you can then change the list's symbol.

We can also indent each of the items in the list. We can increase or decrease the indent. You can get the **Decrease Indent** or **Increase Indent** commands from the paragraphs command group.

Home
Insert
Design
Layout
References
Mailings
Review
View
Help
Cut
Copy
Format Painter
Calibri (Body)
11
ipboard
Font
Paragraph
Off

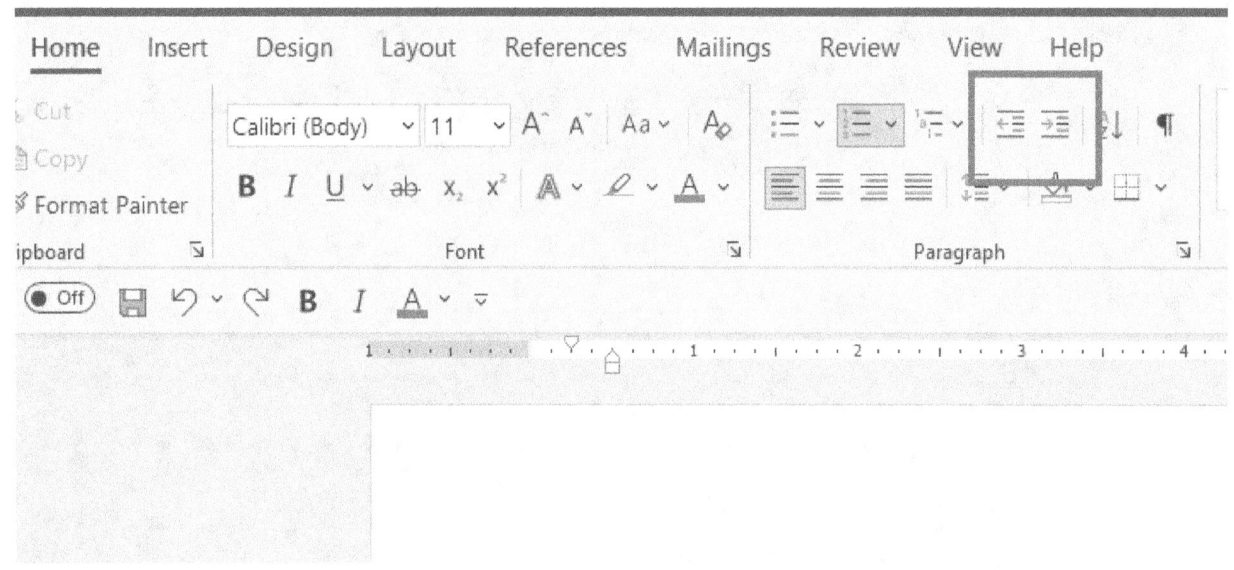

Imagine a document with lists, structured this way, as shown below.

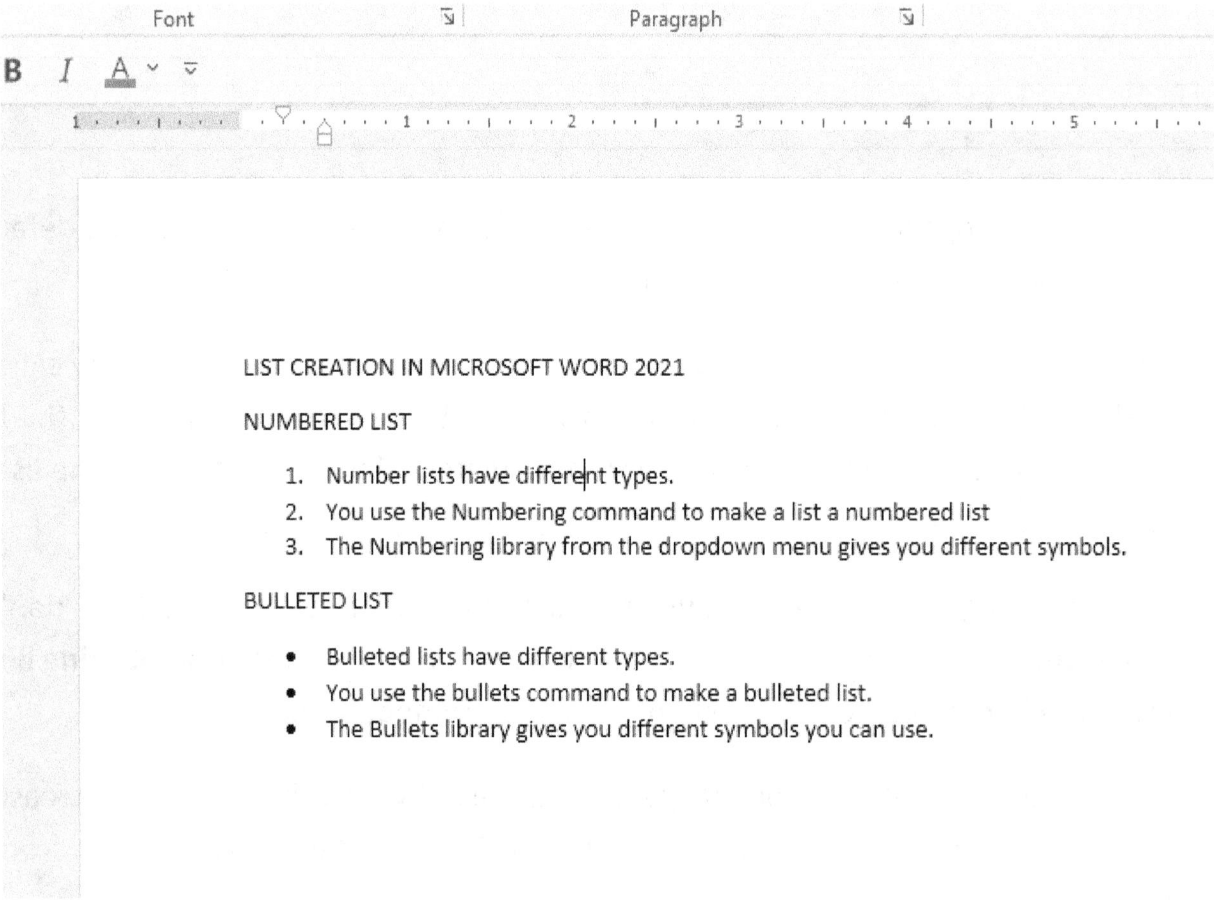

Font
Paragraph
LIST CREATION IN MICROSOFT WORD 2021
NUMBERED LIST
1. Number lists have different types.
2. You use the Numbering command to make a list a numbered list
3. The Numbering library from the dropdown menu gives you different symbols.
BULLETED LIST
• Bulleted lists have different types.
• You use the bullets command to make a bulleted list.
• The Bullets library gives you different symbols you can use.

If I want to move the second items in the numbered list and bulleted list document one-tab inwards, I have to place my cursor at the beginning of those items and click on the increase indent command. They will then appear as below.

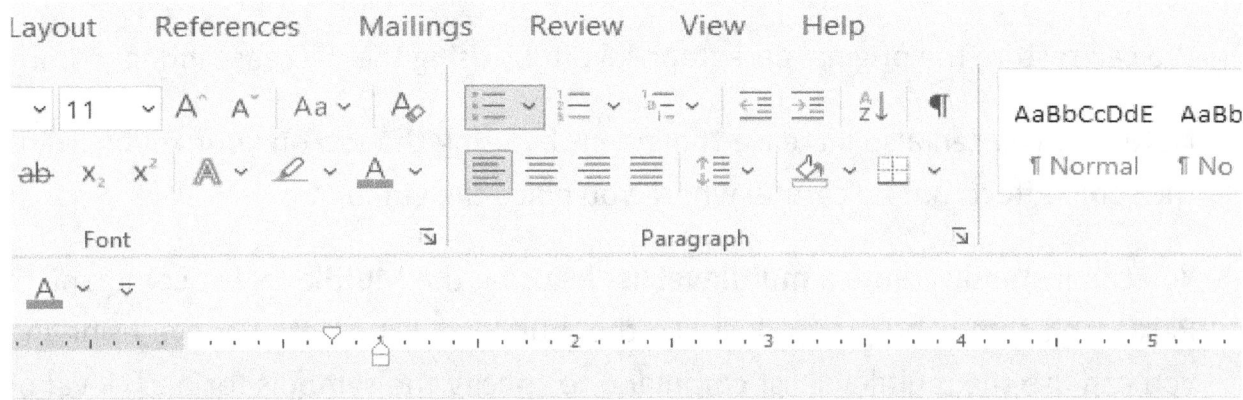

LIST CREATION IN MICROSOFT WORD 2021

NUMBERED LIST

1. Number lists have different types.
    a. You use the Numbering command to make a list a numbered list
2. The Numbering library from the dropdown menu gives you different symbols.

BULLETED LIST

- Bulleted lists have different types.
    o You use the bullets command to make a bulleted list.
- The Bullets library gives you different symbols you can use.

You will notice two things:

1. The symbol for that item that was indented in the list has changed. For the Numbered list, the symbol changed to "a," while for the Bulleted list, the symbol changed to "o."
2. The hierarchy of the items also changed. This has made a list a multilevel list.

You can see now that there is a primary and secondary level for the list.

Try creating a document with a list and practicing the increase indent command yourself.

We can restore the original paragraph layout by using the decrease indent command.

Note that you can also increase the indent by using the tab on your keyboard. It has the same effect. But be careful where you place the cursor.

You can instantly create a **multilevel list** by using the **Multilevel list** command in the **Paragraph** command group. Just like the multilevel list created above using indent, you can use the multilevel list command to specify the symbols for each level of the list.

I can change the first Numbered list in the multilevel list above to use different types of hierarchies. For example, if I chose this template from the multilevel list command:

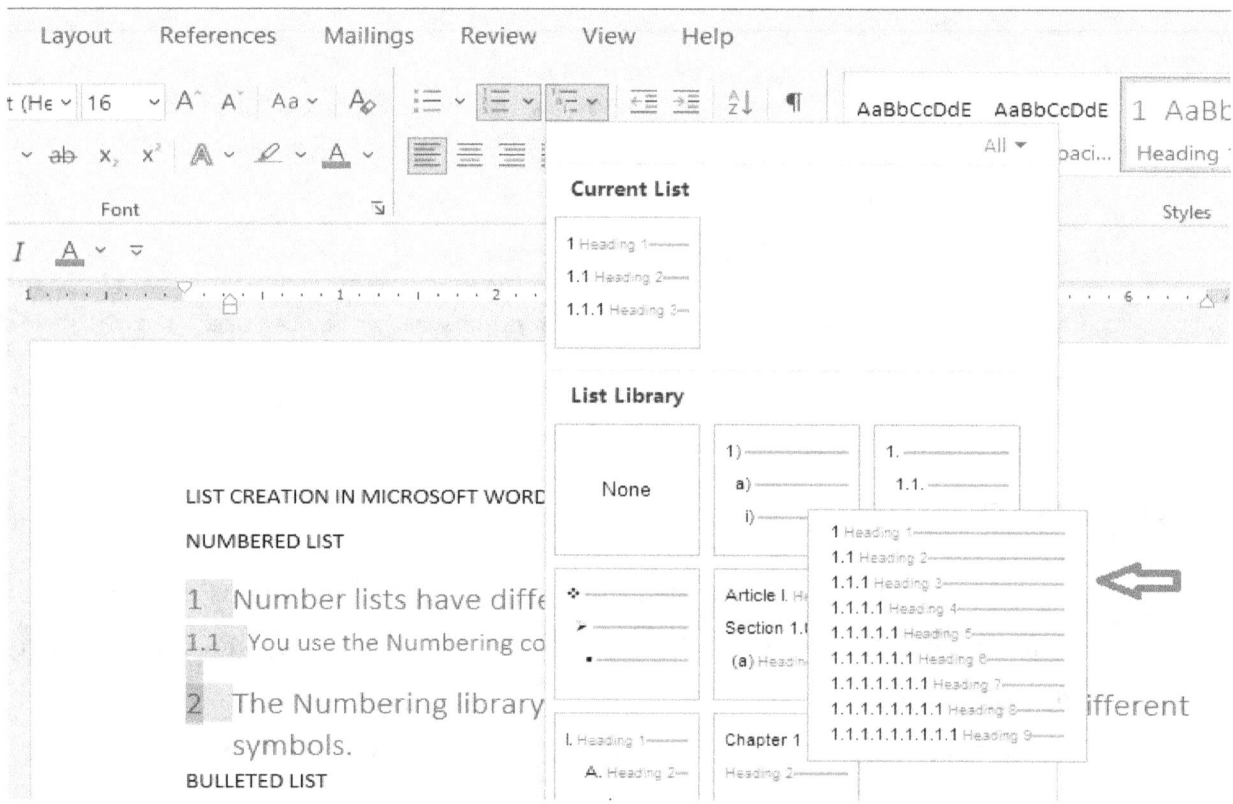

This is how the Numbered list will look. You can see how the multilevel list was customized.

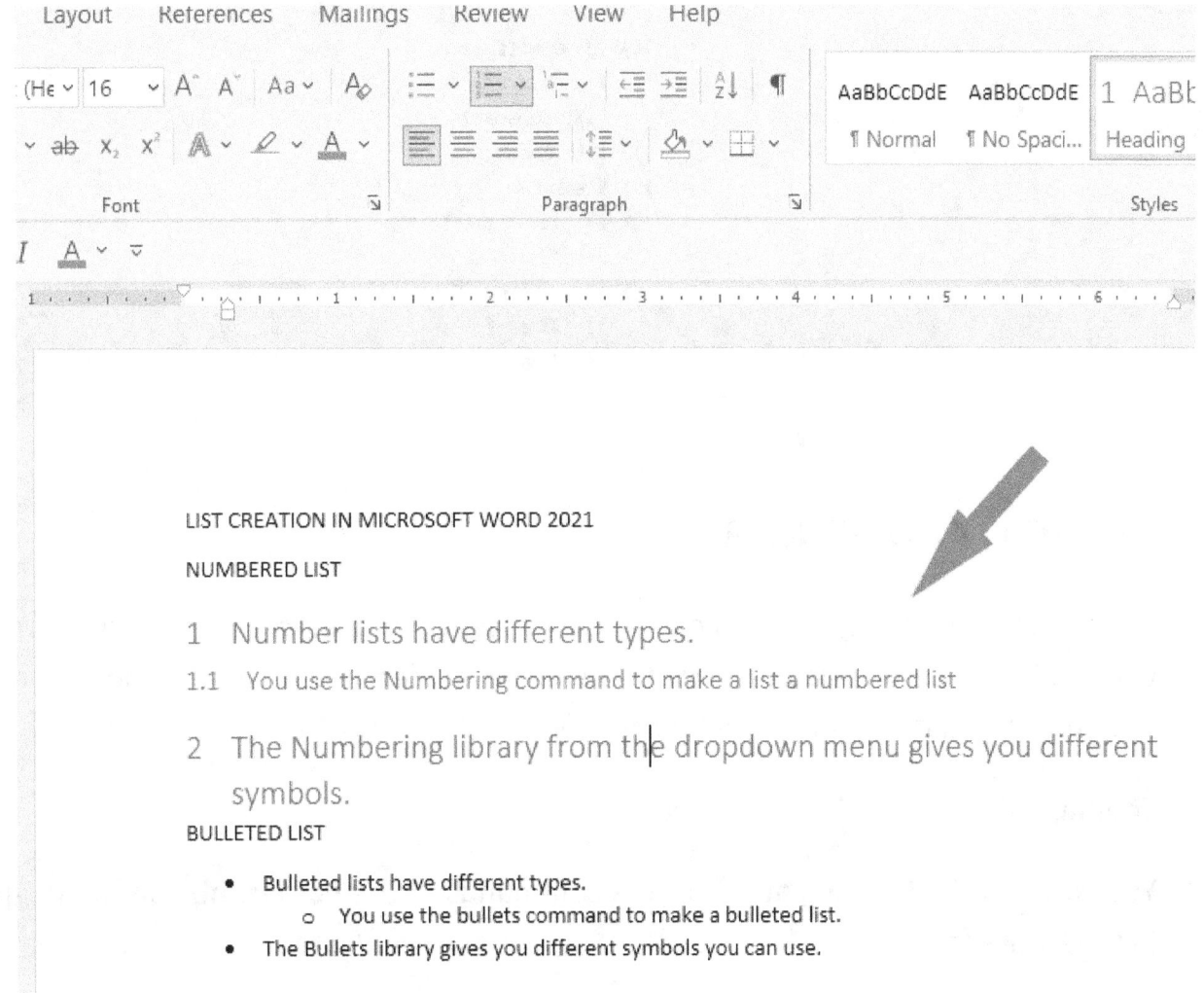

The primary and secondary levels' indicators have changed based on what was chosen from the library.

You can create any level of your multi-level list as long as you can keep the list organized. Let me give you a challenge. Can you create a multi-level list with three levels - primary, secondary, and tertiary - based on what you have learned in this section? Your list should be organized as per the image below.

1) Shopping list
   a) Breakfast.
      i) Eggs
      ii) Bread
      iii) Tea
   b) Lunch
      i) Bacon
      ii) Salad
   c) Dinner
      i) Beef
      ii) Yam

SHADING AND BORDERS

If you want something to stand out in a document, for example, the information you want to highlight, or if you're going to guide the reader's eyes through the document, then borders and shading would be appropriate for doing that.

Shading

You can find the **Shading and Borders** commands in the **Paragraph** command group in the **Home** tab.

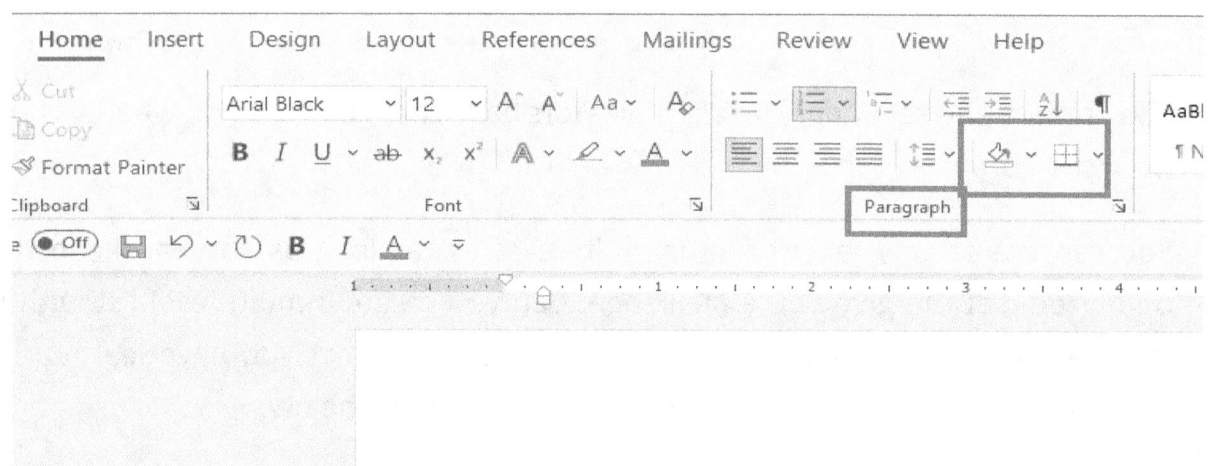

Shading changes the color behind a selected text, table, or paragraph.

For example, look at the selected text below, where a light orange color was applied. What was done was to highlight the text, click on the dropdown for the shading command, and then the preferred color, orange, was chosen. The color was placed behind the text.

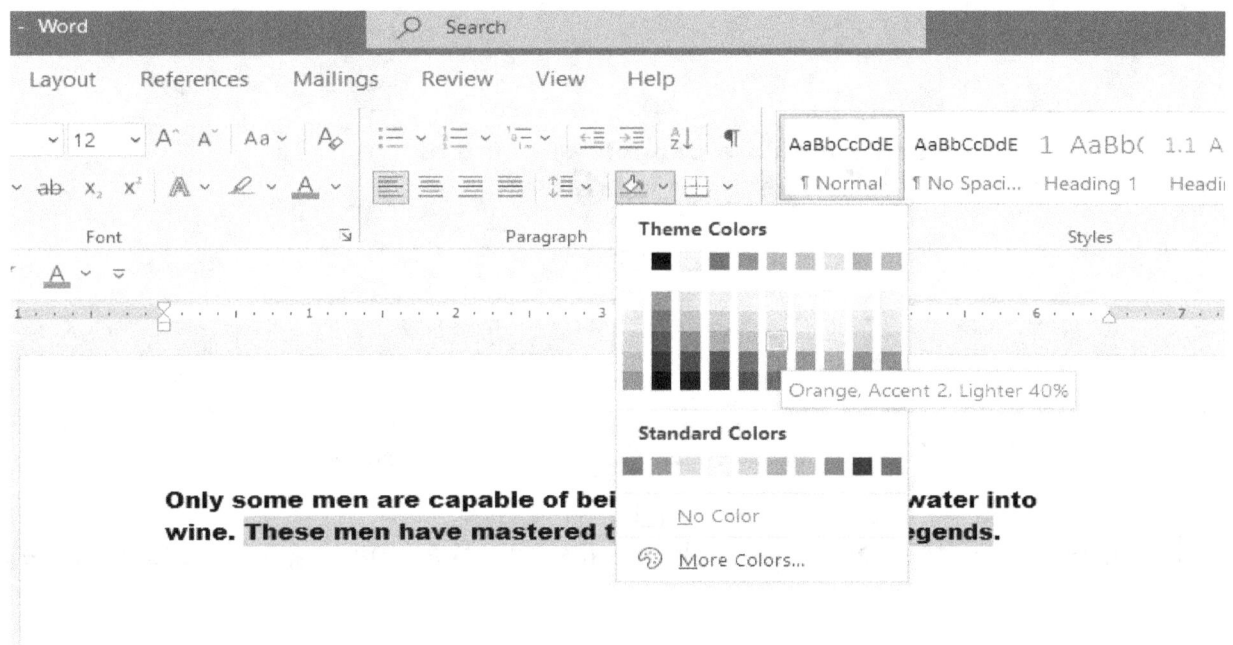

Let's see how we can apply borders to the selected text.

Borders

Note that borders improve the readability of your text by adding variety to the text, and then it helps the eyes by highlighting important visual elements. Borders are usually used for highlighting a table in Microsoft Word, but you can use them on the text in your documents. You can use a border at the top, bottom, left, right, or all sides of the table or text. We will add a border to all sides for the selected text above.

To do so, just select the text that was shaded. Go to the borders command and click the dropdown menu. Then select the **All Borders** option.

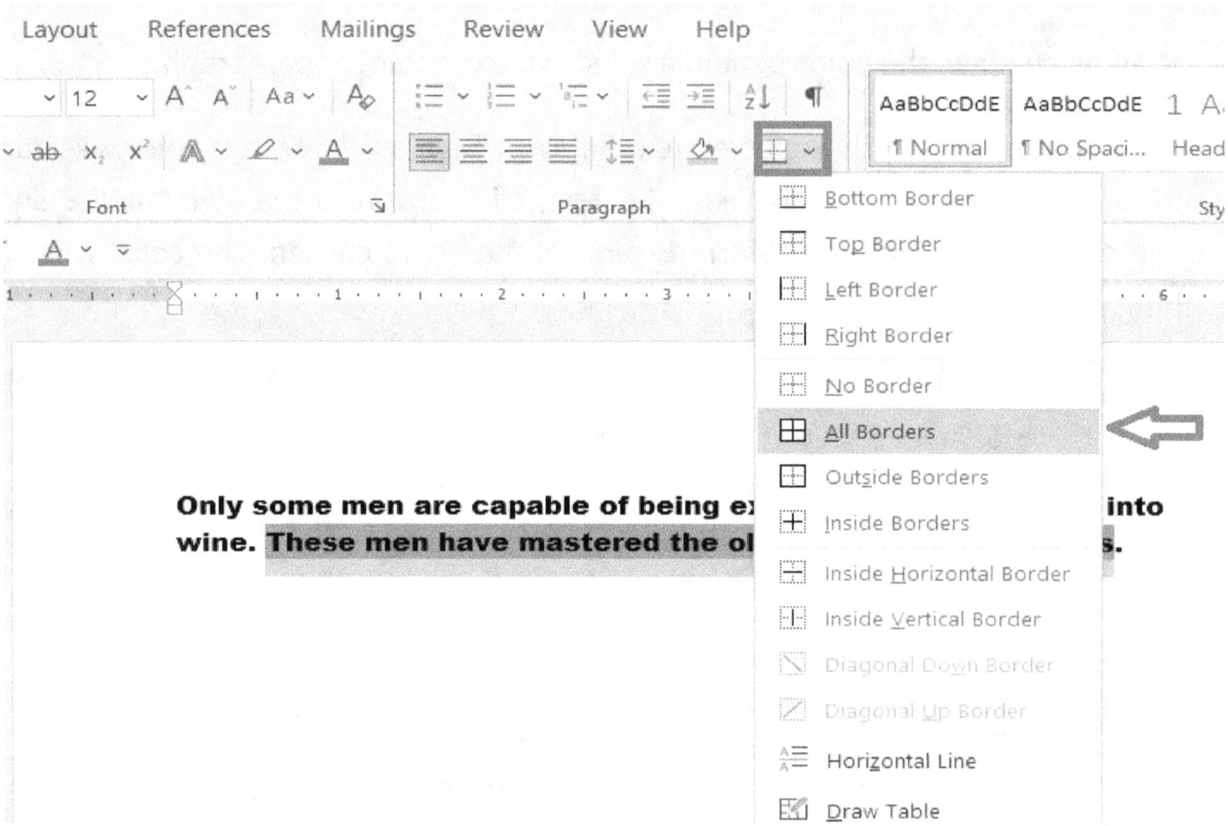

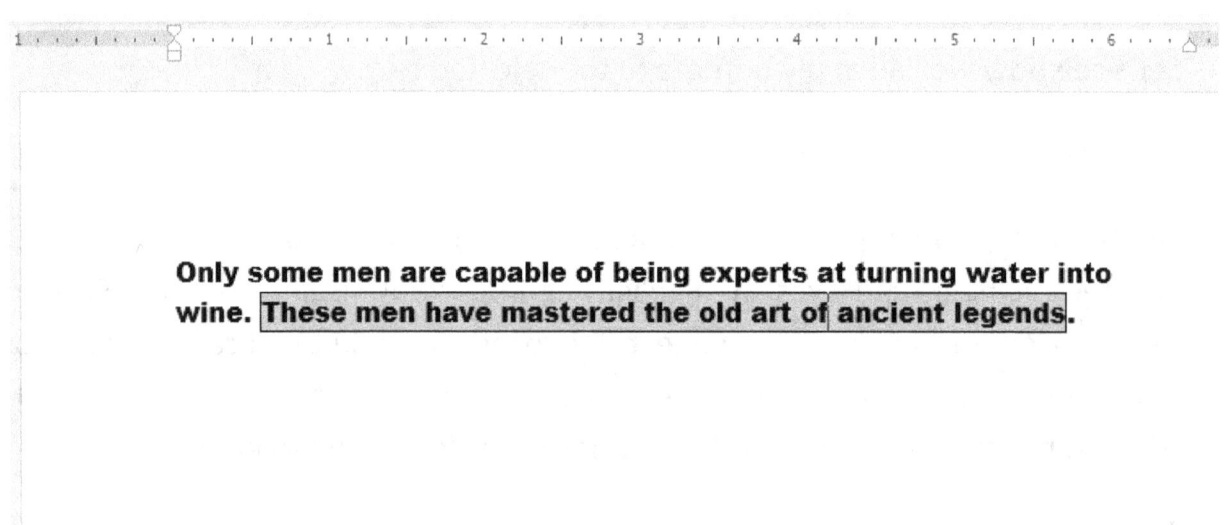

Layout   References   Mailings   Review   View   Help

12   A˄ A˅   Aa ˅   A◇

AaBbCcDdE   AaBbCcDdE   1   A
¶ Normal   ¶ No Spaci...   Head

Font   Paragraph   Sty

⊞ Bottom Border
⊞ Top Border
⊞ Left Border
⊞ Right Border
⊞ No Border
⊞ All Borders   ⇐
⊞ Outside Borders
⊞ Inside Borders
⊟ Inside Horizontal Border
⊟ Inside Vertical Border
◩ Diagonal Down Border
◪ Diagonal Up Border
≡ Horizontal Line
▦ Draw Table

Only some men are capable of being ex   **into wine. These men have mastered the ol**   **s.**

This is now how the selected text looks like now that shading and borders have been applied to it.

Only some men are capable of being experts at turning water into wine. These men have mastered the old art of ancient legends.

Isn't it lovely? You must agree that shading and adding borders to the selected text makes it visually appealing and attractive.

I urge you to practice shading and borders. Create some text and choose any shading and border you prefer. Show the final product to your friends.

This chapter highlights simple techniques to automate some of your work in Microsoft Word. With these, you can go on to adopt other ones with experience.

FORMAT PAINTER AND STYLES

The format painter helps us to work more efficiently. Using this tool, you can apply different formats at once to a document. For example, you can quickly apply the same formatting for size, color, and font style to multiple pieces of text or graphics. Take the format painter as a copy-and-paste tool for formatting. Using it, the same formatting can be copied from one part of the document to another part of the document.

On the other hand, the styles tool is similar to the format painter but different. The styles tool is a pre-defined style for formatting commands shipped with Microsoft Word. The formatting features pre-defined for a given style are usually more than those you find in the format painter. A given style in the styles command group can include styles for headers, sub-headers, font, size, colors, and font size in the body of text.

You can find the format painter in the **Clipboard** command group and the predefined styles in the **Styles** command group under the **Home** tab.

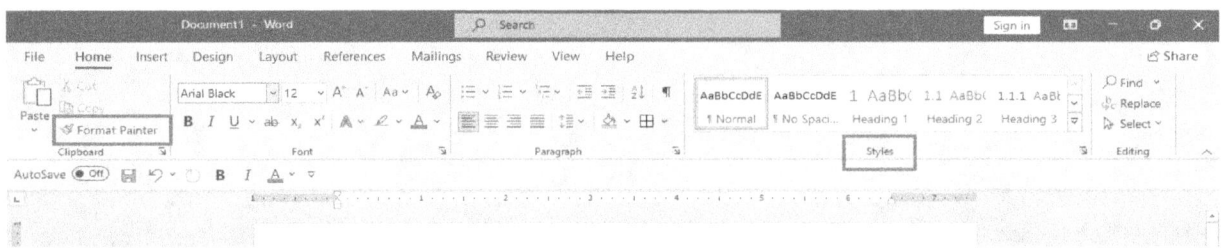

Format Painter

Let's start with a document having three paragraphs like the image below to show you how to apply the format painter.

There are a lot of significant events happening around the world. For example, in 2022, the world saw the collapse of many economies due to the war in Ukraine and rising inflation rates. Many would say that the war in Ukraine, where Russia invaded Ukraine, was the cause of the rising inflation rates that saw the collapse of many economies. But that is not the case.

Since 2020, the start of the Covid-19 pandemic, the world has been held to a standstill economically due to fears about the impact on significant economies of the pandemic. Many people were laid off, and factories were not producing anything. Emerging economies like Russia and China were greatly hit by the effects of the pandemic.

That is why experts posit that rather than the war in Ukraine bringing about the global rise in inflation around the world, the pandemic that started the rise in inflation might have been the stimulus to the war in Ukraine.

I will apply the following formatting to the first paragraph: **Bold, Font size 14, Font Color Blue**, and all in **italics**. Create your paragraphs so you can follow along.

What we will do next is to select the formatted first paragraph and then click the **Format Painter**. What happens is that Microsoft Word copies the formatting of the formatted paragraph. Then, we have to hover over the paragraph to which we want to apply this copied formatting. Let's make it the third paragraph. A **paintbrush** now appears. Using the paintbrush, select the third paragraph.

Immediately after finishing the selection, the formatting of the first paragraph is applied to the third paragraph.

Here is the image of the final result.

There are a lot of significant events happening around the world. For example, in 2022, the world saw the collapse of many economies due to the war in Ukraine and rising inflation rates. Many would say that the war in Ukraine, where Russia invaded Ukraine, was the cause of the rising inflation rates that saw the collapse of many economies. But that is not the case.

Since 2020, the start of the Covid-19 pandemic, the world has been held to a standstill economically due to fears about the impact on significant economies of the pandemic. Many people were laid off, and factories were not producing anything. The effects of the pandemic greatly hit emerging economies like Russia and China.

That is why experts posit that rather than the war in Ukraine bringing about the global rise in inflation around the world, the pandemic that started the rise in inflation might have been the stimulus to the war in Ukraine.

The first and third paragraphs now have the same formatting. Isn't that cool and efficient? It saves you the time of manually redoing what has already been applied to the first paragraph on the third paragraph.

You will notice that after applying the formatting from the format painter to the third paragraph, the copied formats needed to be recovered. If you want to apply this to several paragraphs, double-click the format painter instead of clicking it once, and it will preserve the formatting so it can be applied to multiple paragraphs. When you're done, uncheck the format painter by clicking the **Format Painter** command.

Styles

The **Styles** command group will help us simultaneously apply the same predefined formats to a document. For example, let's say I have a document like the one below, and I want to apply the same predefined heading style to all the headers.

Paragraph 1 Header

There are a lot of significant events happening around the world. For example, in 2022, the world saw the collapse of many economies due to the war in Ukraine and rising inflation rates. Many would say that the war in Ukraine, where Russia invaded Ukraine, was the cause of the rising inflation rates that saw the collapse of many economies. But that is not the case.

Paragraph 2 Header

Since 2020, the start of the Covid-19 pandemic, the world has been held to a standstill economically due to fears about the impact on significant economies of the pandemic. Many people were laid off, and factories were not producing anything. The effects of the pandemic greatly hit emerging economies like Russia and China.

Paragraph 3 Header

That is why experts posit that rather than the war in Ukraine bringing about the global rise in inflation around the world, the pandemic that started the rise in inflation might have been the stimulus to the war in Ukraine.

I will highlight all the text meant to be paragraph headers. Head over to the styles command group, and then click on **Heading 1**. Immediately, all the paragraph headers are formatted with the same styling.

1   Paragraph 1 Header

There are a lot of significant events happening around the world. For example, in 2022, the world saw the collapse of many economies due to the war in Ukraine and rising inflation rates. Many would say that the war in Ukraine, where Russia invaded Ukraine, was the cause of the rising inflation rates that saw the collapse of many economies. But that is not the case.

2   Paragraph 2 Header

Since 2020, the start of the Covid-19 pandemic, the world has been held to a standstill economically due to fears about the impact on significant economies of the pandemic. Many people were laid off, and factories were not producing anything. The effects of the pandemic greatly hit emerging economies like Russia and China.

3   Paragraph 3 Header

That is why experts posit that rather than the war in Ukraine bringing about the global rise in inflation around the world, the pandemic that started the rise in inflation might have been the stimulus to the war in Ukraine.

You can also find the headers in the navigation pane. Remember the navigation pane?

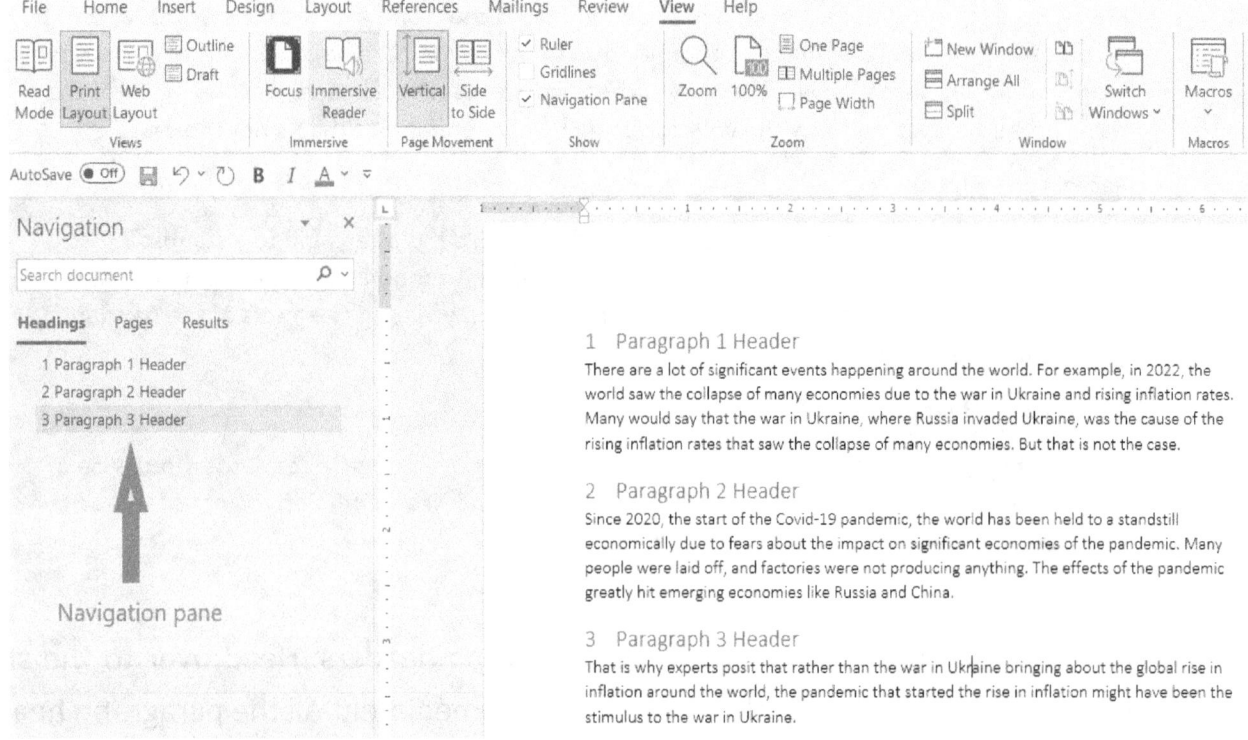

You can navigate to each header by clicking its entry on the navigation pane.

Now you know how to use the format painter and styles command. Go ahead and try them out yourselves. You will notice how efficient they make you.

MANAGING LISTS

Remember when we created headers from our lists with the **Styles** command group? Creating headers in a large document in this manner allows you to collapse and expand the headers and their contents. This is particularly useful if you are working on a large document.

For example, imagine we have the headers and lists as below:

MY MENU FOR TODAY

BREAKFAST
- Tea
- Bread
- Eggs

LUNCH
- Bacon
- Yam
- Salad

DINNER
- Rice
- Stew
- Beef

Breakfast, lunch, and dinner are headers with subcategories as lists. We can now collapse or expand each header by hovering the mouse over the header. When you hover the mouse over a header, you get a little arrow sign like this.

MY MENU FOR TODAY

BREAKFAST
- Tea
- Bread
- Eggs

LUNCH
- Bacon
- Yam
- Salad

DINNER
- Rice
- Stew
- Beef

On clicking on each of the arrows, the header and all its contents collapse instantly. Try to click on the arrows for the three headers, and you will get a document that looks like this.

MY MENU FOR TODAY

▶ BREAKFAST
▶ LUNCH
▶ DINNER

On clicking again, you expand the headers, and they return to how they were initially.

Another way you can manage lists is to sort lists. You can sort a numbered or bulleted list of one level by going to the sort command. The sort command can be found in the **Home** tab under the **Paragraph** command group.

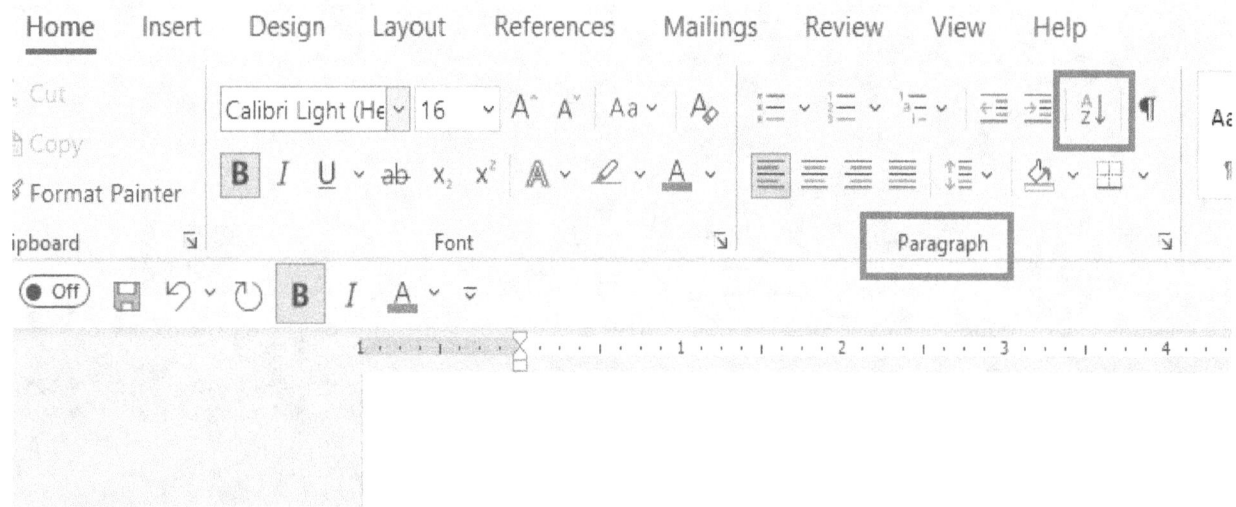

Now taking our initial list of menus, let's sort each item. To sort a list, you just have to do the following:

1. Select/Highlight the list.
2. Go to the **Sort** command that can be found in the **paragraph** command group under the **Home** tab.
3. A dialog box will now appear. From the dialog box, choose how you want to sort the list by. It could be either by **paragraph**, **headings**, or **field**. We will use headings for now.
4. Choose whether you want to sort it by ascending or descending order. Ascending order starts from A-Z (lowest number to highest), and descending order starts from Z-A (highest number to lowest).
5. Choose **OK**. Your list is now sorted.

We'll now choose all the lists in the document as outlined above. Then sort by paragraphs and click in ascending order. We will get a document that looks like the image below.

MY MENU FOR TODAY

BREAKFAST
- Tea
- Bread
- Eggs

DINNER
- Rice
- Stew
- Beef

LUNCH
- Bacon
- Yam
- Salad

You will notice that the order of the headings has changed. "**D**" comes before "**L**," so "**Lunch**" has been moved to third place while "**Dinner**" has moved to second place. "**Breakfast**" still retains its initial position because "**B**" comes before "**D**" and "**L**."

What if we sort by headings and in descending order? Can you guess what the order of the headings will be? This is what it will look like.

MY MENU FOR TODAY

LUNCH
- Bacon
- Yam
- Salad

DINNER
- Rice
- Stew
- Beef

BREAKFAST
- Tea
- Bread
- Eggs

You should create a series of lists and headers and then try sorting them. It's great fun.

Apart from sorting texts, we can also sort numbers and dates. Let's try out some examples with sorting dates.

For example, we have some dates structured this way.

MY DAILY CALENDAR

DAYS
- 1/12/2023
- 1/10/2023
- 1/08/2023
- 1/15/2023
- 1/07/2023

Let's sort it in ascending order. That is, from the latest date with the earliest date at the bottom. You will notice that when you select the dates list, Microsoft Word immediately recognizes the items in the list as a date. You have to choose the paragraph type when sorting because the list of dates is not a header or a field.

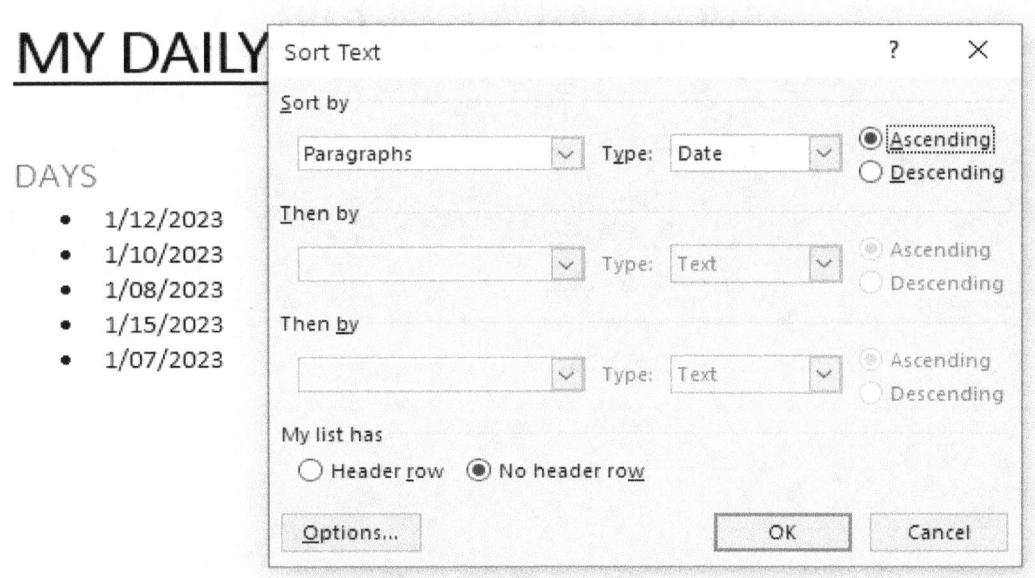

After clicking **OK**, the dates are rearranged this way.

MY DAILY CALENDAR

DAYS
- 1/07/2023
- 1/08/2023
- 1/10/2023
- 1/12/2023
- 1/15/2023

As an exercise, recreate the dates and try sorting them by descending order. This is what you should get in your document.

MY DAILY CALENDAR

DAYS
- 1/15/2023
- 1/12/2023
- 1/10/2023
- 1/08/2023
- 1/07/2023

Other Ways to Manage Lists

Let's look at other ways we could manage lists. When you have a list, you can right-click inside the list, and a menu gives you several options for managing the list.

We can use this menu to **Adjust list indents** or even use **Separate List** to separate the list. We can change the Font, paragraph type, and other facts about the list.

Let's try out adjusting list indents. On clicking this option, another dialog box appears.

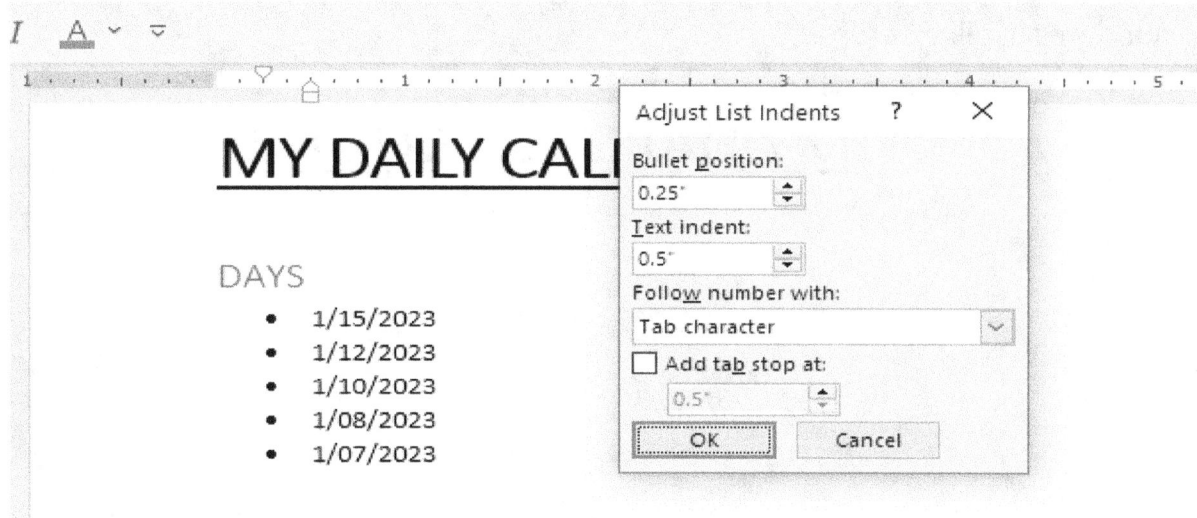

We can see that we can change the **bullet position**, adjust the **text indent**, or choose how to follow the number, or even specify where the tab stop should be. Let's adjust the bullet position to 1 inch, and you will see that the tab stops for the bullets will shift forward to place the bullets deep down inside the document.

MY DAILY CALENDAR

DAYS
- 1/15/2023
- 1/12/2023
- 1/10/2023
- 1/08/2023
- 1/07/2023

Compare the bullet position of this image with the earlier image to compare the effect of adjusting the bullet position. There is now a separation in the list in the document. Play around with other options in the dialog box, and you will see what powerful features Microsoft Word has for managing lists.

There is also a numbering trick I would like to show you. For example, let's start with our dates list like before.

MY DAILY CALENDAR

DAYS
1. 1/15/2023
2. 1/12/2023
3. 1/10/2023
4. 1/08/2023
5. 1/07/2023

I want to start renumbering the list at the 4th position so that the list will start at one in this position. We right-click on the list at that 4th position and select **Continue numbering**. A power button will appear.

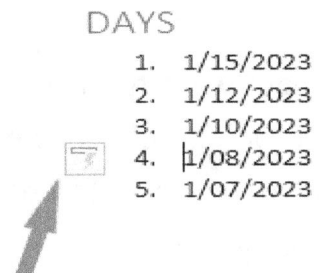

DAYS
1. 1/15/2023
2. 1/12/2023
3. 1/10/2023
4. 1/08/2023
5. 1/07/2023

Click on the dropdown for this button. Then choose **Restart Numbering.** That fourth position will restart its numbering from 1 to give a list that looks like this.

MY DAILY CALENDAR

DAYS
1. 1/15/2023
2. 1/12/2023
3. 1/10/2023
1. 1/08/2023
2. 1/07/2023

You can see how the numbering stops at 3 and then restarts.

We have many options for managing lists that space and time will not allow us to cover in this guide. Go ahead and experiment with each of the options. You learn by practicing.

There are several reasons someone might want to insert a table to a document. For example, instead of presenting data in paragraphs as we have been doing, a table might be a more effective way to make data more structured and visually appealing. Tables can also be used for text and number alignment. Tables can be used to compare data, create charts, and make graphs. Many people use a table to create columns for text and images.

This lesson will show you that creating a table gives you more options in terms of formatting, so you don't have to worry about line breaks and tab stops. We will consider various ways to create a table and manipulate it.

DRAWING A TABLE

The command for the tables can be found at the **Insert** tab on the **Tables** command group.

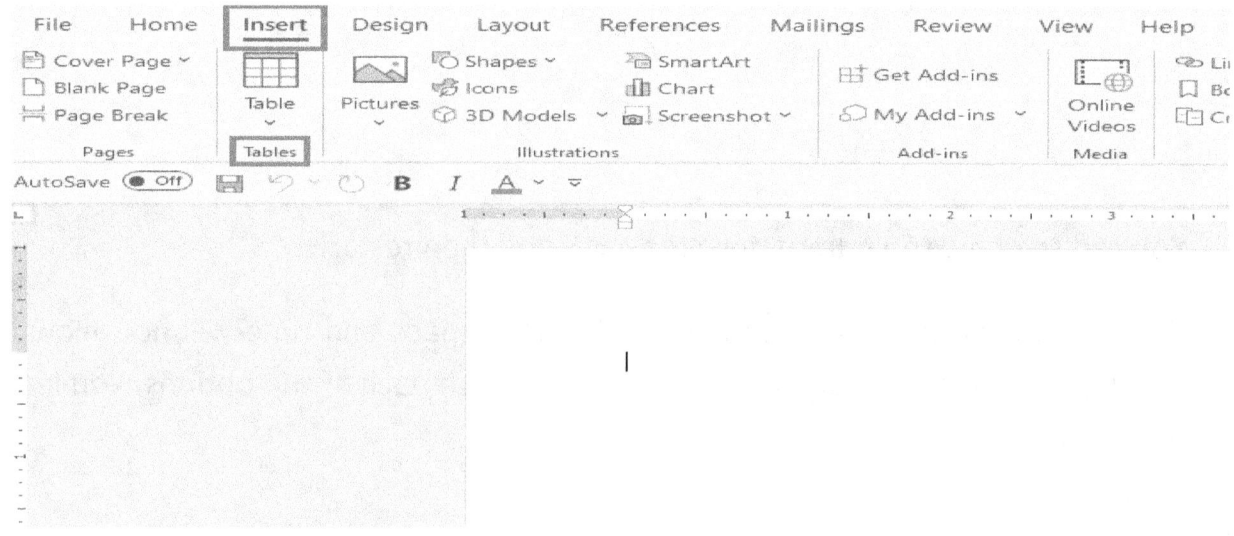

There are several ways we can insert a table. The first is through the drop-down menu on the **Table** command. You will instantly see an option to Insert a Table with several boxes. The boxes represent the rows and columns for the table. Choose the number of rows and columns you want using your mouse, and you will instantly see the preview on the document.

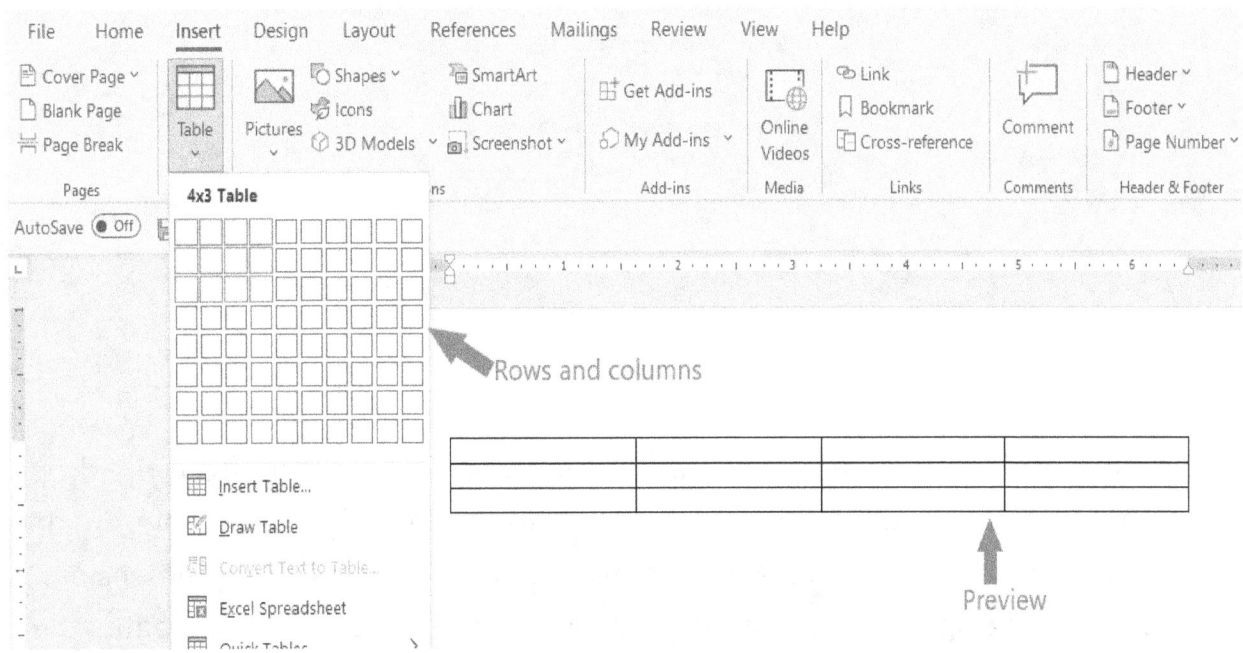

From the image above, you can see that 4 columns and 3 rows were selected by using my mouse, and the preview was shown instantly on the document. When I click on the mouse, the table is instantly created.

You should create various tables using this method. Create a 2 by 3 table and then a 5 by 5 table.

Another way to create a table is to use the **Insert Table** option from the dropdown menu. When you click this option, you get a dialog box where you specify the number of columns and rows you want to create in the table. You can also specify if you want the table to autofit to the document content or the document window. When you click the **OK** button, the table is instantly created.

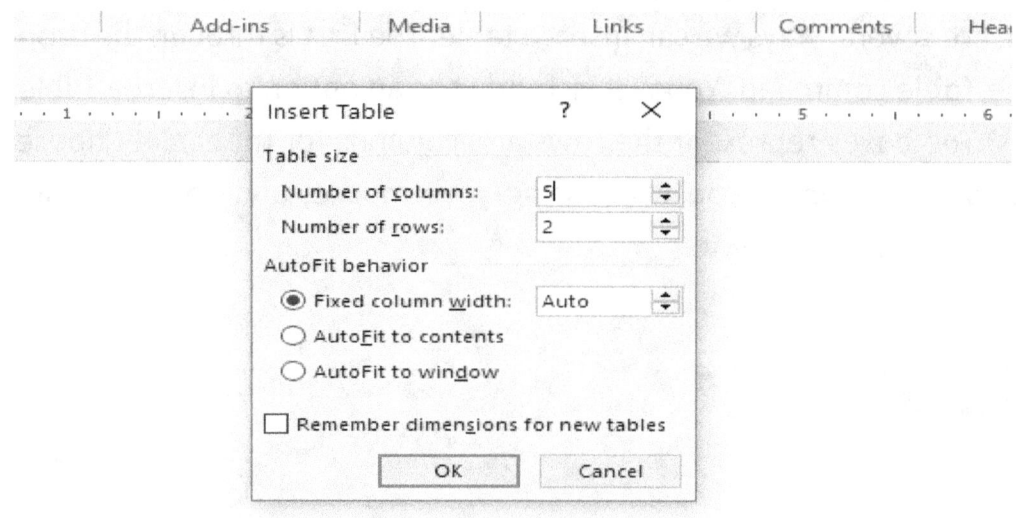

Another way to create a table is to use the **Draw Table** option from the dropdown menu. This option gives you greater flexibility in designing your table. By drawing them, you can use them to specify irregular tables and tables of any dimension. When you draw it using a provided virtual pen, Microsoft Word instantly creates the table and aligns all the cells. The image below shows an irregular table created using the **draw table** option in the table dropdown menu.

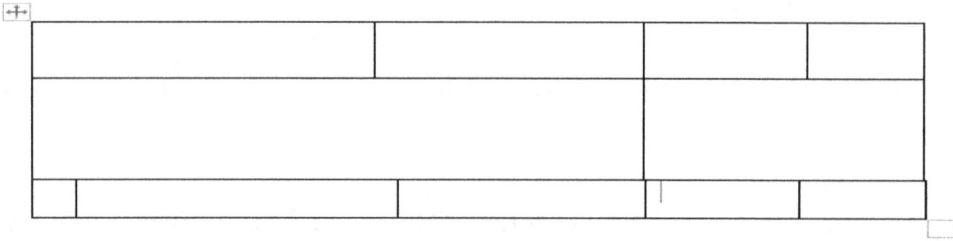

As always, to be effective in any of these tools, you must practice using them. So, right now, practice the three methods for creating tables.

This is a tip for adding new rows to an already existing table. Just place your cursor at the last cell to add new rows to your created table. Then click on the **Tab** button on your keyboard. Instantly, Microsoft Word will create a new row with the specifications of the last row.

TABLE DESIGN AND LAYOUT

All tables have a contextual menu. That's one cool thing with Microsoft products, including Microsoft Word. Immediately you create a table, a contextual menu appears, as seen in the image below. The contextual menu has tabs for the **Table Design** and **Table Layout**.

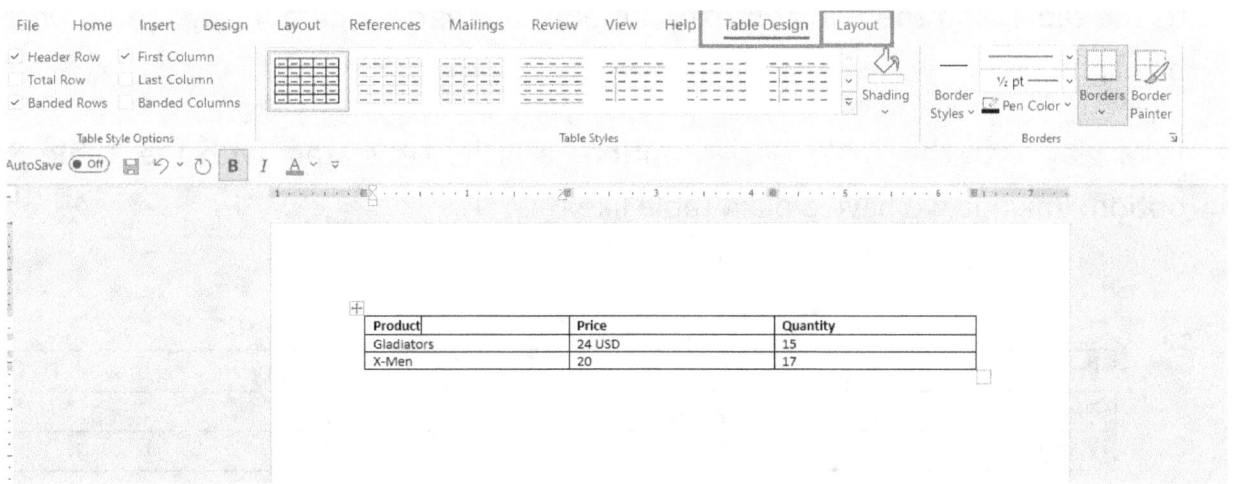

The **Table Design** contextual menu has 3 command groups: **Table Style Options, Table Styles**, and **Borders**.

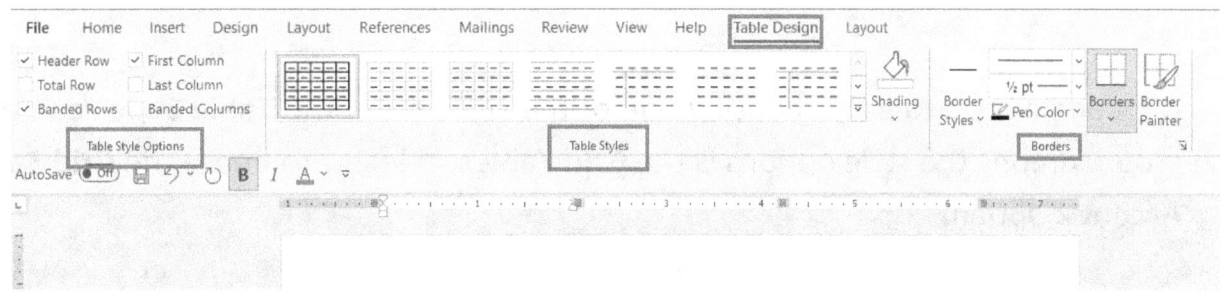

The contextual **Layout** menu has more command groups. They include **Table, Draw, Rows, Columns, Merge, Cell Size, Alignment,** and **Data**.

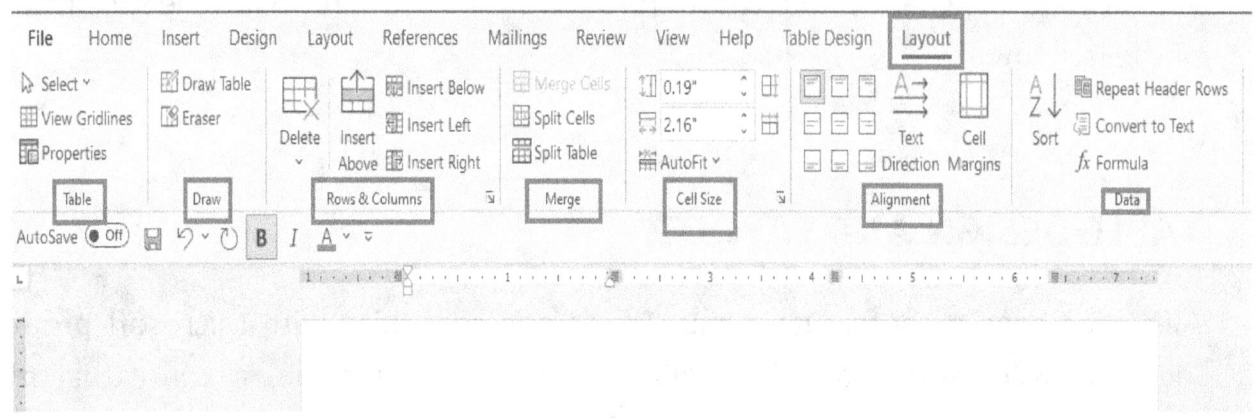

You will notice that if you click away from the table, the menu goes away. Click back to the table, and the two contextual menus appear. By default, the Table Design is highlighted.

Let's play with the Table Design options a little. Let's start with the **Table Styles** option. Imagine we have a plain table like this.

Product	Price	Quantity
Gladiators	24 USD	15
X-Men	20	17

Let's add a style to it by choosing one of the styles from the **Table Styles** command group. Among the style options is the **Grid Tables** style. I will choose the **Grid Table 4 Accent 2** option.

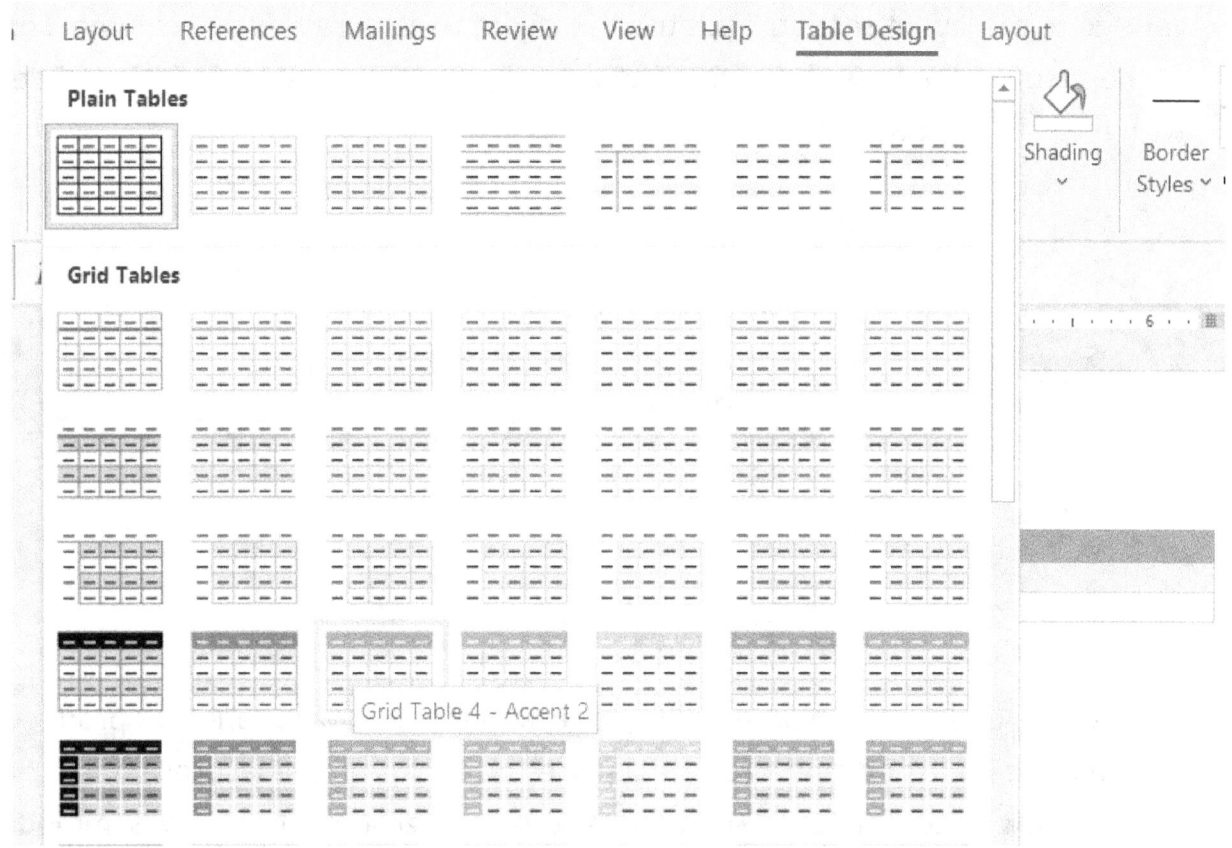

It will give us an elegantly styled table that looks like the image below:

Product	Price	Quantity
Gladiators	24 USD	15
X-Men	20	17

As an exercise, you can try out several styles to see how the table styling commands work. Microsoft Word gives you several options that make your tables visually appealing. You can try out list tables or even plain table styles.

Let's go to the layout section. Let's use the layout to insert a row and column. For this, we need to use the **Rows & Columns** command groups. For example, let's say we start with the table below.

Product	Price	Quantity
Gladiators	24 USD	15
X-Men	20	17

We want to add a new column called rating and a new row for another product. The first thing to do to add a new row is to place the cursor on the last row. Then click on **Insert Below** under the **Rows & Columns** command group. A new row is immediately inserted below the last row. We could also insert above or below any row. Just choose the appropriate command. Then to insert the column, you first place the cursor on the last column. Then click **Insert Right** to insert a new column to the right of the last column.

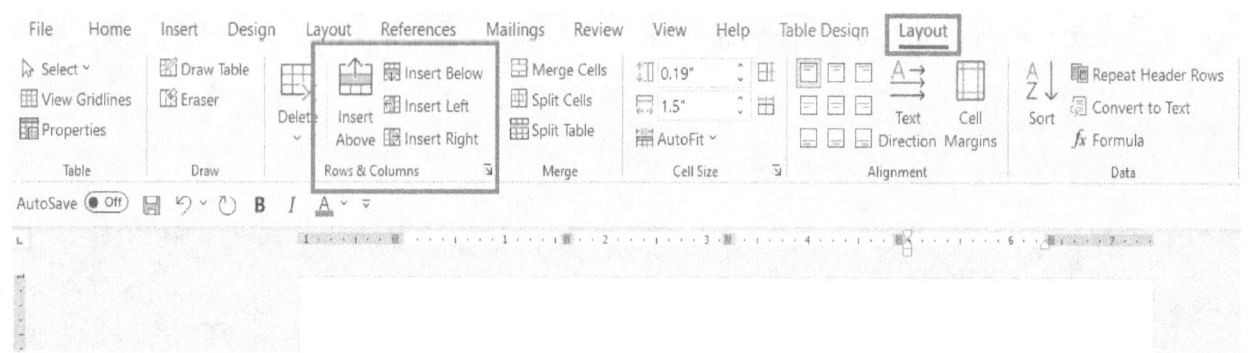

As with inserting new columns, you could insert a new column to the left or right of the current cursor column. The appropriate command is there.

After inserting the rows and columns, you now fill in the values of the table so that the table might probably appear this way.

Product	Price (USD)	Quantity	Ratings
Gladiators	24	15	4
X-Men	20	17	5
The Force	30	35	3

Looking at the table above, you will see that our table doesn't have a title. Let's give it a title. We need to create a top row for that. I want you to figure out how to create the top row. It's simple. Just place your cursor on the first row and then click on **Insert Above** under the **Rows & Columns** command group. A new top row is instantly created. Let's give the row a name for the title. Something like a "**Product listing**" will be adequate.

We have a table like this;

Product Listing			
Product	Price (USD)	Quantity	Ratings
Gladiators	24	15	4
X-Men	20	17	5
The Force	30	35	3

Merging cells

If you look carefully, you will see that the title row has four separate cells, and the title is in the first cell. We need the title to be at the center of the row. To do that, we need to merge the four cells and then center the title. How do we merge cells?

You can find the command to merge cells under the **Merge** command group in the **Layout** tab when the table is highlighted. To begin merging cells, select all the contiguous cells to be merged. In this case, the four cells of the title row. After selecting them, click on the **Merge Cells** command in the **merge** command group. The cells are immediately merged.

To center the title, we go to the **Home** tab this time, and under the **Paragraph** command group, you need to click on the **Center** command.

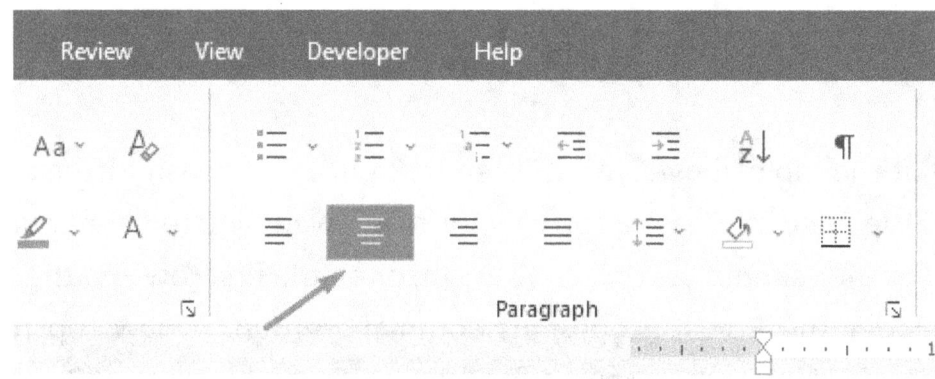

That's it. Our table now looks like the image below.

Product Listing			
Product	Price (USD)	Quantity	Ratings
Gladiators	24	15	4
X-Men	20	17	5
The Force	30	35	3

A quick tip: Can you quickly resize the columns and rows with your mouse? Yes, you can. Just hover over the borders in a table for the column or row you want to resize, and a crosshairs sign will appear. Move the crosshairs sign to increase or decrease the size of the rows and columns.

Table Borders

You can change the border of your table to make it look more visually appealing. You will notice that our table doesn't have borders. We can fix that. First, select the table. Then on the **Table Design** tab, go to the **Borders** command group. Click on the dropdown menu for the **Borders** command. You will find different types of borders to apply to the table. We will choose the **All Borders** option. That is, all the rows and columns will now have a border. The table will end up looking like the image below.

Product Listing			
Product	**Price** (USD)	**Quantity**	**Ratings**
Gladiators	24	15	4
X-Men	20	17	5
The Force	30	35	3

In retrospect, instead of adding borders to the table, you could choose specific rows, columns, or cells to which you want to apply a border. Just select that row, column, or cell.

Converting a Table to Text

One last practice we'll now do is to convert the table to text. Then from text back to a table.

To convert a table to text, we need to first select the table. Then under the **Layout** tab and the **Data** command group, click on the **Convert to Text** command.

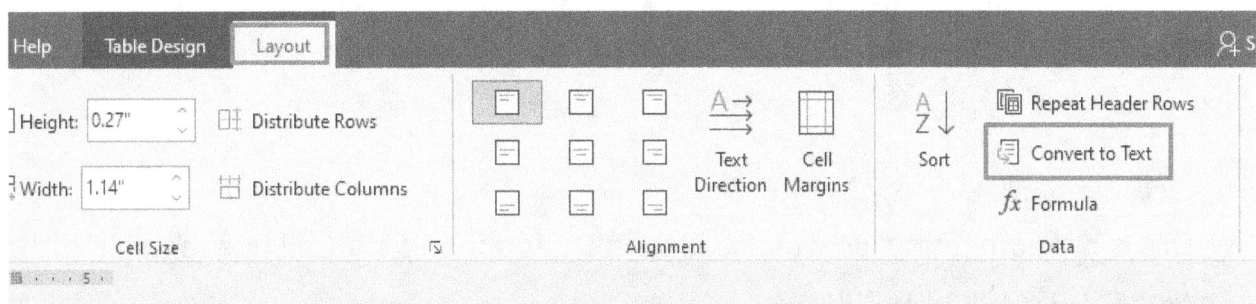

You will get options like the following:

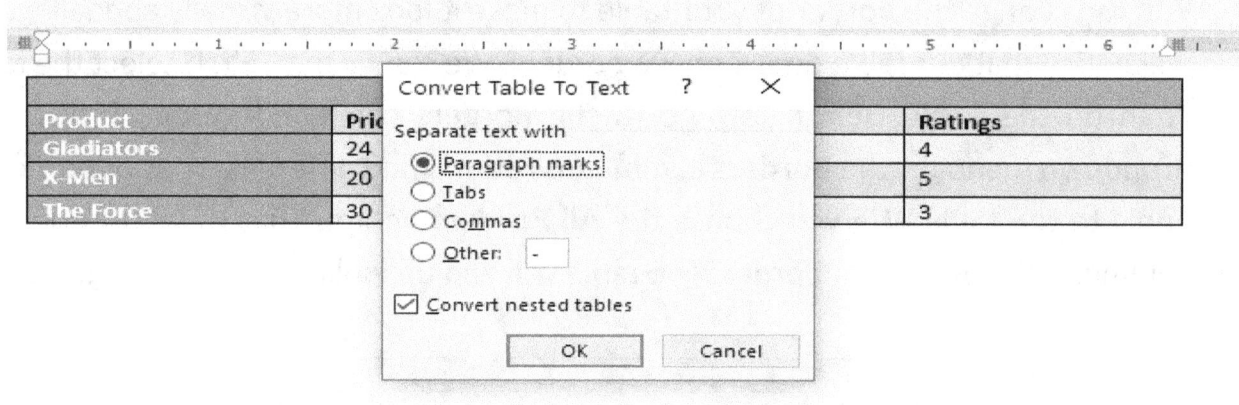

Let's see how the text will look with the **Paragraph marks** option.

This is not something we can use. So, let's undo it and start all over again. This time, we'll choose the tabs option.

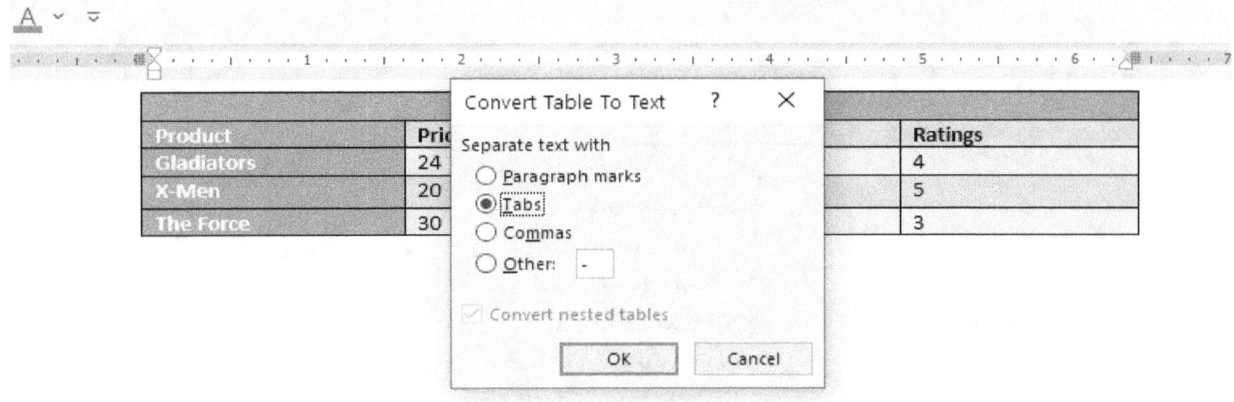

Product	Price			Ratings
Gladiators	24			4
X-Men	20			5
The Force	30			3

This gives us a text that is like this:

Product Listing

Product	Price (USD)	Quantity	Ratings
Gladiators	24	15	4
X-Men	20	17	5
The Force	30	35	3

This text is much better.

We can convert the text back to a table. To do that, you have to select the text above. Then, go to the **Insert** tab, and under the **Tables** command group, you click the dropdown menu for tables. Then select **Convert Text to Table.** A dialog box like this appears.

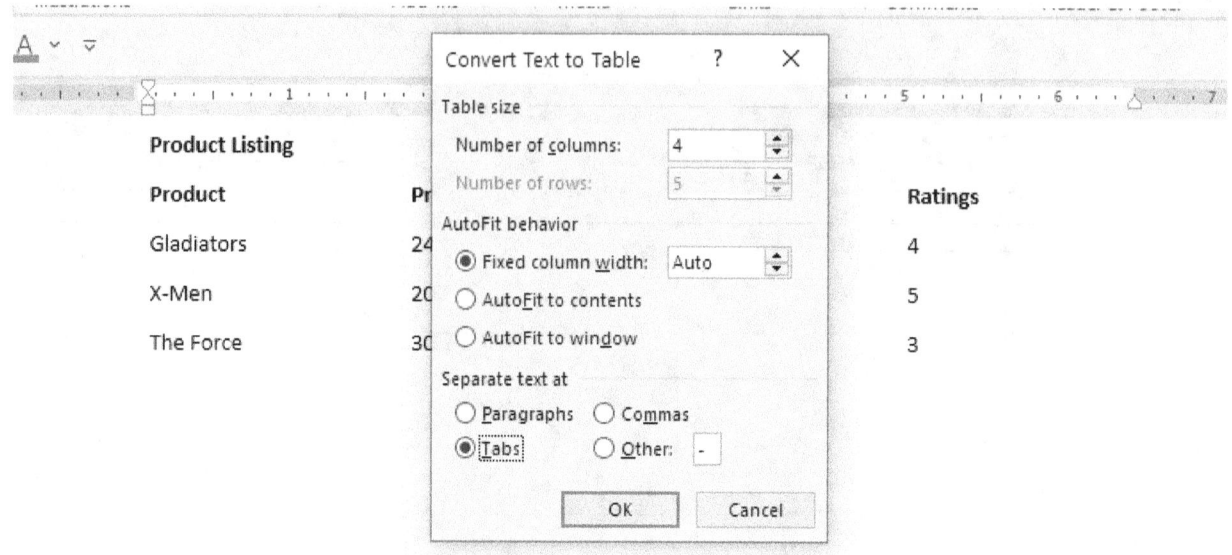

Under the **Separate text at** section, choose **tabs**, and Microsoft Word will immediately insert the table size. Then click OK. You will now get back to your table.

Product Listing			
Product	Price (USD)	Quantity	Ratings
Gladiators	24	15	4
X-Men	20	17	5
The Force	30	35	3

That's it. What you get is a plain table. You can style it and apply other manipulations to the table using what we practiced above.

You might have noticed that graphics make a document easier to understand. A document with graphics is lively and visually appealing compared to a document without graphics. You must have noticed that this guide has lots of graphics or images. Without them, you would not be able to understand most of what is being described.

ADDING GRAPHICS

On Microsoft Word, you can add graphics from the **Insert** tab, and the **illustrations** command group. Check the image below.

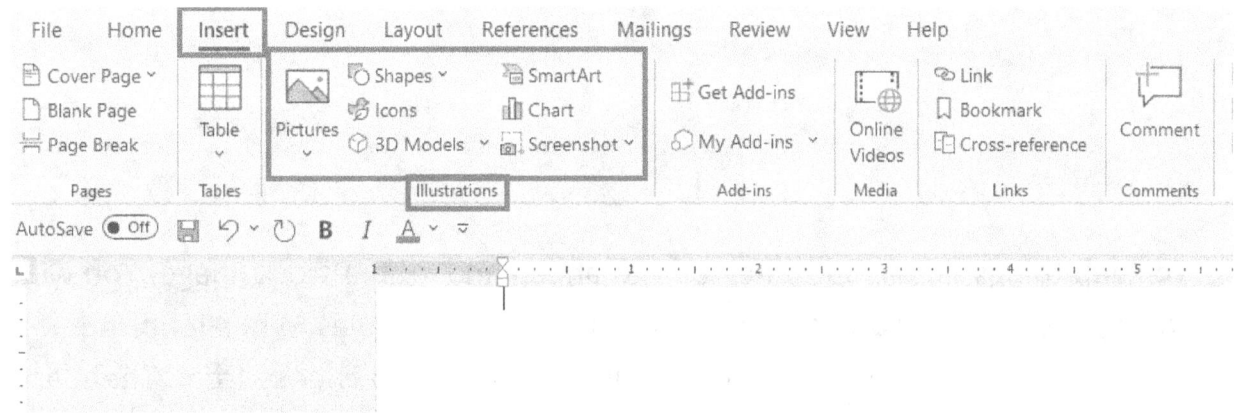

Some of the graphics you can add include **pictures, shapes, icons, 3D Models, SmartArt, Charts**, and **Screenshots**.

You can insert images using the **Pictures** command in the **Illustrations** command group. When you click on the Pictures dropdown icon, you can see several options for inserting pictures. They include the ability to insert pictures from:

- **This device**: With this option, you can insert any picture in your computer or laptop.
- **Stock image**: These images come bundled with Microsoft Word. The library of stock images keeps expanding by the day and is copyright-free.
- **Online Pictures**: With this option, you can search for images online, choose any, and it is instantly inserted into your Word document.

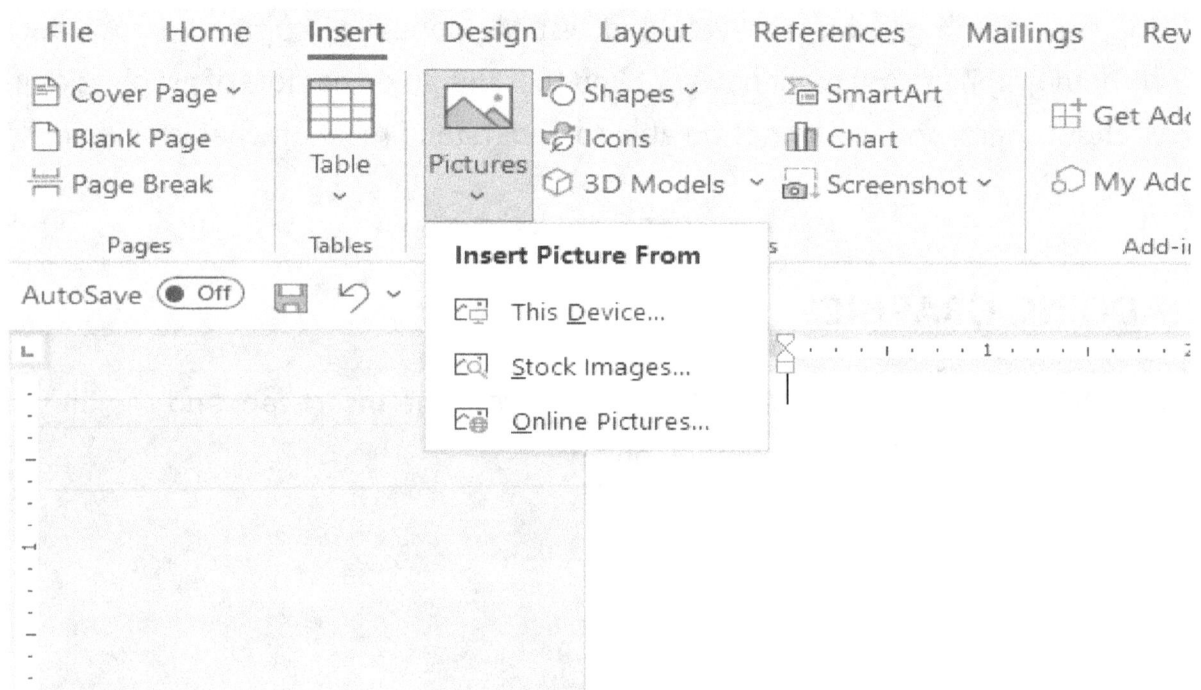

To keep things simple and safe, let's go ahead and grab a stock image. You will have to be patient as the software needs to load the stock images. When it finishes loading, you will see that you have many stock image options to choose from. There are tabs for **Images, Icons, Cutout people, Stickers, Illustrations**, and **Cartoon People**. The world of stock images is immense. When you scroll down, you will notice that there are tons and tons of images to choose from in each category.

You will see that you are on the **Image** tab on **Stock Images**. You can search for different types of images. Some options for image categories include **Winter, Industry, Paper** and etcetera. The options are lengthy.

Let's move over to the Icon tab. You will notice that there are some fabulous icons with categories like **Apparel, Tools and Buildings, Signs and Symbols**, etcetera. We even have some education icons in the mix.

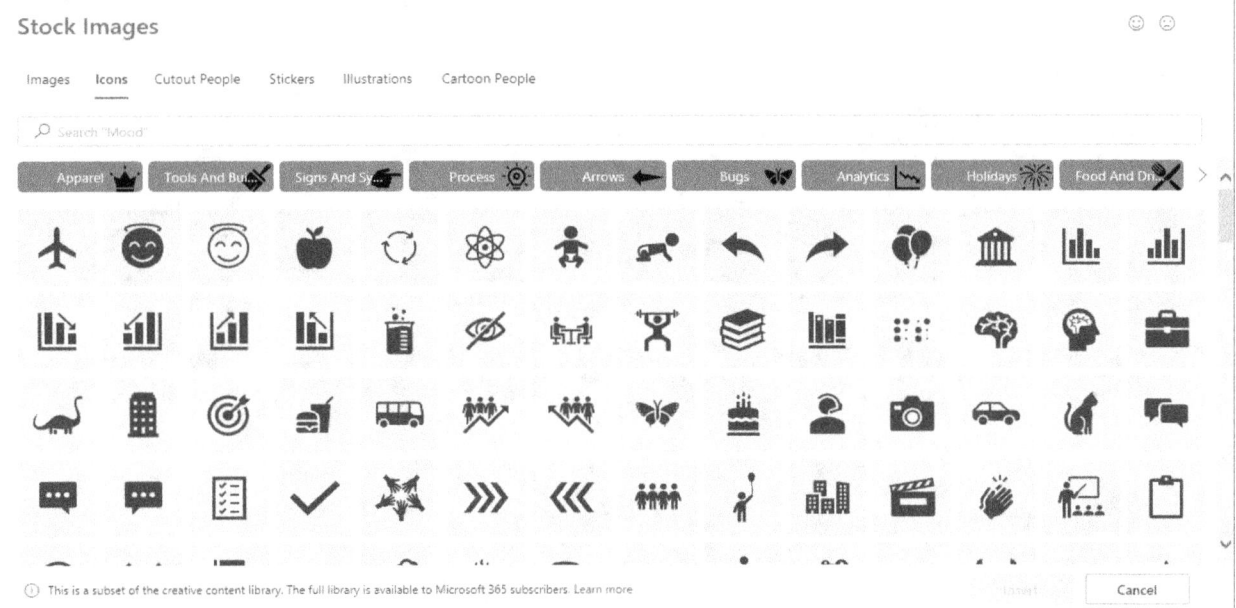

Now let's take a look at some **Cutout People**. We can see lots of really funny people here with different reactions. You can see that they are cutouts of people with different personalities. You can scroll down to see lots of cutouts.

The next tab are the **Stickers**. I think the stickers are pretty fun.

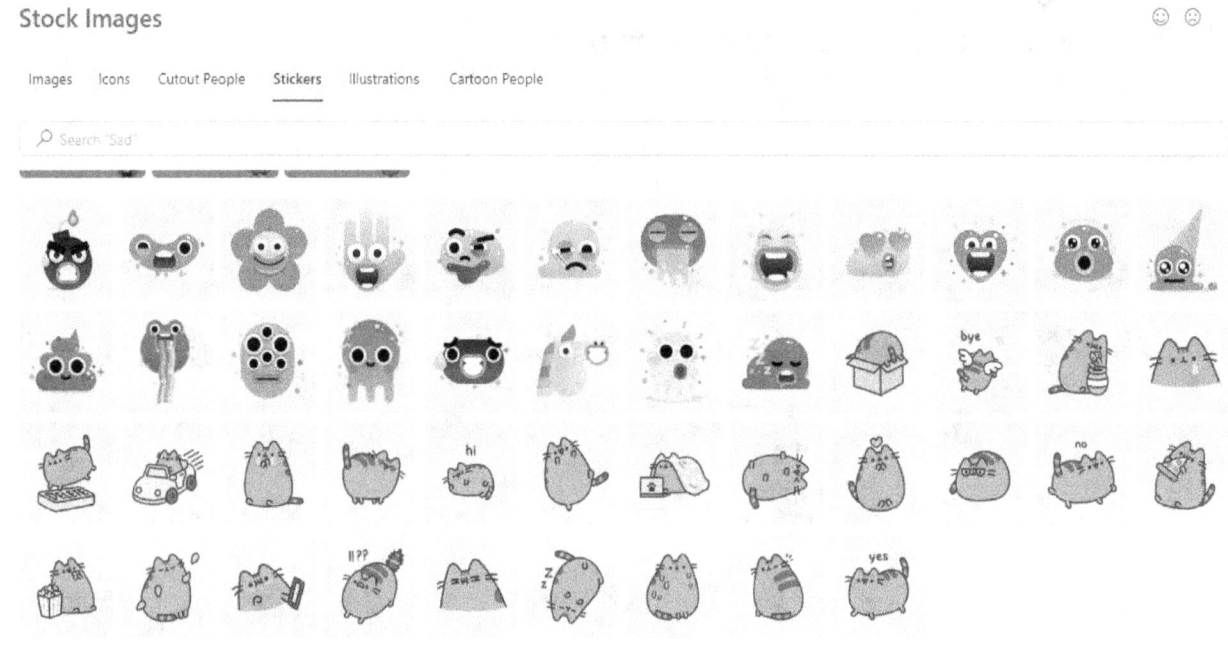

You can explore the rest of the tabs, like the **Illustrations** and **Cartoon People** tab.

Microsoft Word has enabled you to use various graphics in your documents, all available to you at no charge. Using these graphics is as simple as going to each tab or searching for them in the search box in the **Stock Images** dialog box.

Let's practice inserting one of these images into a document.

- Choose an image from the Stock image or search for what you want. For this exercise, I will search for "**flowers**" and choose one of the flowers.
- Click on the image or images you want to use in the document.
- You will notice that immediately you click on an image, an **Insert** button appears at the bottom right.
- When you are done picking images, click on the **Insert** button.
- The image or images are instantly inserted into your document.

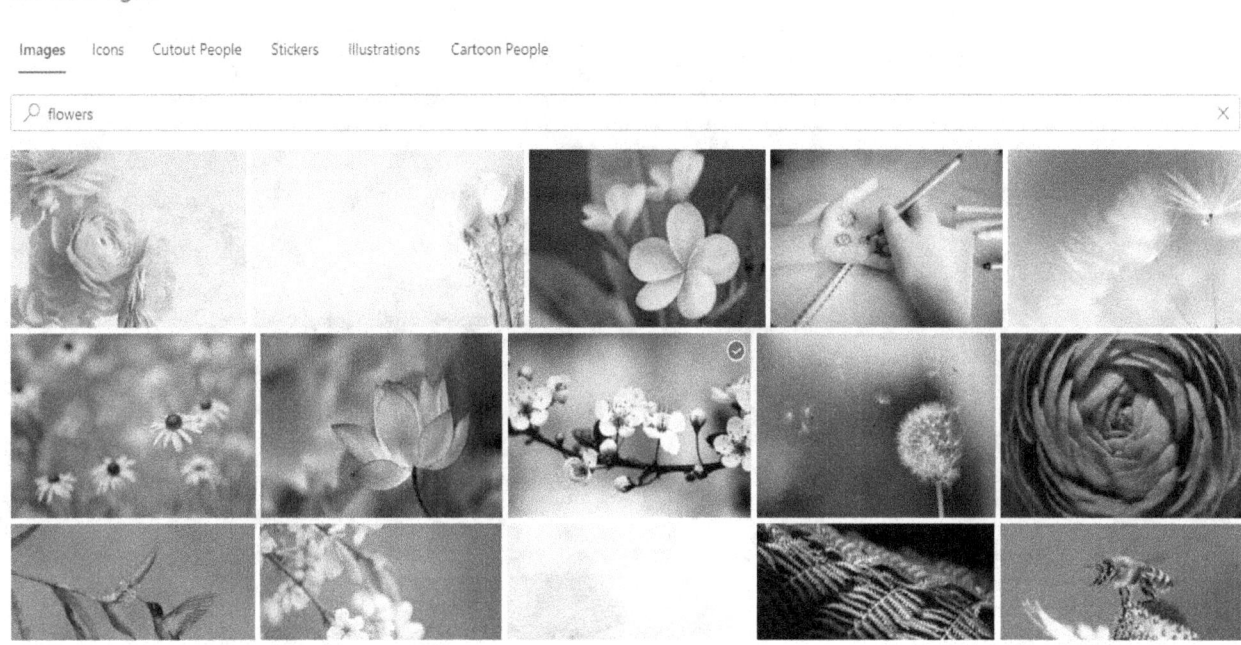

Resizing an Image

The first thing you want to do when you have an image in your document is to resize it. This is because the image size might be larger than what you want in the document. When you have an image inserted into your document, you will find that it has image handles. These are little circles at the sides and edges of the image when you click on the image.

While resizing your images, don't resize them from the handles at the side. This will have an impact on the aspect ratio of your image. Instead, resize it at the corners. There are four corners and sides on an image. Use only the corners to resize your images.

There is a feature in an image that determines the layout of the image with the surrounding text. This is seen when you move an image. The layout feature is located at the upper right side of the image when you click on it.

This is an image at the bottom. It was picked from the stock images in Word 2021. The image is an image of a tree with its flowers. This is an image at the bottom. It was picked from the stock images in Word

Layout options

2021. The image is an image of a tree with its flowers.

This is an image at the bottom. It was picked from the stock images in Word 2021. The image is an image of a tree with its flowers.

This is an image at the bottom. It was picked from the stock images in Word 2021. The image is an image of a tree with its flowers.

The default layout option is **Inline With Text**. That is why you see the text surrounding the image at the top and bottom when you move the image.

If you change the option to **Square**, the text now rests at the side of the image based on how large the image is.

This is an image at the bottom. It was picked from the stock images in Word 2021. The image is an image of a tree with its flowers. This is an image at the bottom. It was picked from the stock images in Word 2021. The image is an image of a tree with its flowers.

This is an image at the bottom. It was picked from the stock images in Word 2021. The image is an image of a tree with its flowers.

This is an image at the bottom. It was picked from the stock images in Word 2021. The image is an image of a tree with its flowers.

If you change the option to **Through**, the text wraps on both sides.

This is an image at the bottom. It was picked from the stock images in Word 2021. The image is an image

of a tree with the bottom. It images in image of a

This is an picked from 2021. The with its

This is an picked from 2021. The with its flowers.

wers. This is an image at icked from the stock Word 2021. The image is an tree with its flowers.

image at the bottom. It was the stock images in Word image is an image of a tree flowers.

image at the bottom. It was the stock images in Word image is an image of a tree

You can practice with different text and image layout options to get a fitting one. The option I use most frequently is the **top and bottom** feature which makes some text to be at the top and some at the bottom based on how you move the image.

nThis is an image at the bottom. It was picked from the stock images in Word 2021. The image is an image of a tree with its flowers. This is an image at the bottom. It was picked from the stock images in Word 2021. The image is an image of a tree with its flowers.

This is an image at the bottom. It was picked from the stock images in Word 2021. The image is an image of a tree with its flowers.

This is an image at the bottom. It was picked from the stock images in Word 2021. The image is an image of a tree with its flowers.

Another feature of the image handle is that we can rotate the image. The rotation feature is at the top of the image when you click on it. Here I have rotated the image with the rotation feature.

Rotation

nThis is an image at the bottom. It was picked from the stock images in Word 2021. The image image of a tree with its flowers. This is an image at the bottom. It was picked from the stock in

Picture Format

Images have contextual menus. When you click on any image, you get a contextual menu called **Picture Format.**

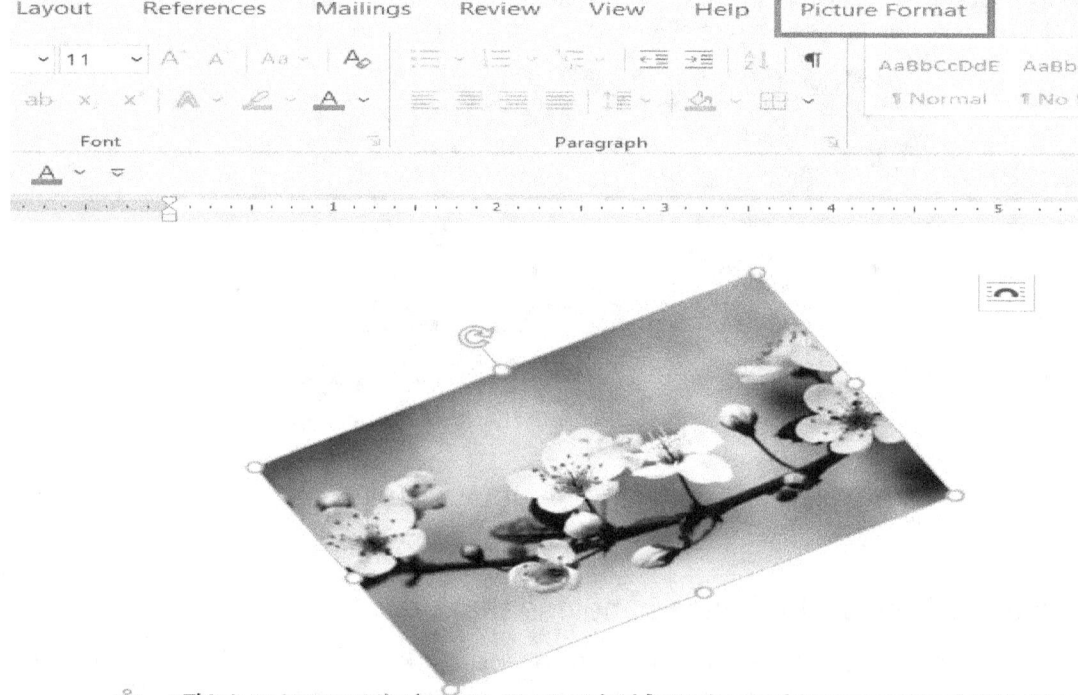

nThis is an image at the bottom. It was picked from the stock images in Word 2021. The i image of a tree with its flowers. This is an image at the bottom. It was picked from the st

The Picture Format contextual menu gives you several options for formatting images. These are the same tools that are available in other Microsoft products.

Using the **Picture Format** contextual menu, you can remove the background from an image. You can apply various color corrections and shades using the **Corrections** command in the **Adjust** command group. We can also recolor the images using the **Color** command.

Here is the image above recolored.

nThis is an image at the bottom. It was picked from the stock images in Word 2021. T
image of a tree with its flowers. This is an image at the bottom. It was picked from the
Word 2021. The image is an image of a tree with its flowers.

This is an image at the bottom. It was picked from the stock images in Word 2021. Th
of a tree with its flowers.

You can also give artistic effects to an image. This will make it look more like a sketch or painting.

Word 2021. The image is an image of a tree with its flowers.

This is an image at the bottom. It was picked from the stock images in Word 20
of a tree with its flowers.

If you notice you have made too many changes, you can always reset the picture. The **Reset Picture** command is in the **Adjust** command group under the **Picture Format** contextual menu. Look for it. I reset the picture above and got back my original picture.

Word 2021. The image is an image of a tree with its flowers.

This is an image at the bottom. It was picked from the stock images in Word 202: of a tree with its flowers.

We can also add accessibility options to the picture using the **Alt Text** command. You can find the **Alt Text** command under the **Accessibility** command group. This is useful for screen readers. Go ahead and try it out.

The **Picture Styles** command group is one feature you'll love and use a lot. With this command, you can change the overall look of your picture. Let's try out an example.

I can choose a **beveled oval black** look for the picture.

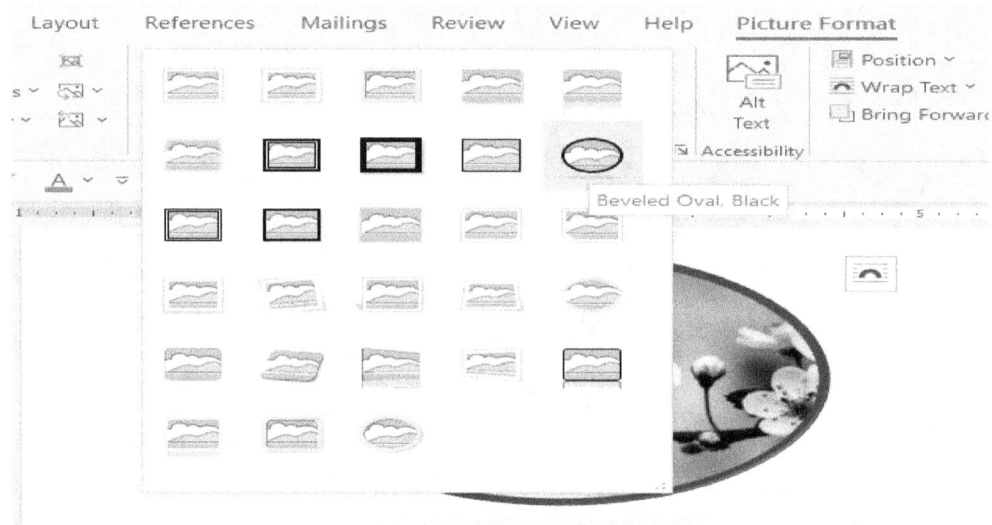

This is what the picture now looks like. Oval with a black shadow underneath.

nThis is an image at the bottom. It was picked from the stock images in Word 2021. The

Isn't this beautiful?

There are lots of features and options under the **Picture Format** contextual menu. I encourage you to interact with them and try them out to get a feel for what they can do on an image. I have only covered the basics. You can find other options like positioning the image, selecting the transparency, and cropping it to a desired size. The more you practice, the more advanced your Microsoft Word knowledge and skills will improve.

INSERTING SYMBOLS AND CHARACTERS

Let's go back to the **Insert** tab. In earlier chapters, we were able to insert a few things so far. We have already learned how to insert a table and also how to insert a picture. But there are other symbols we would need to learn to insert. If we move over to the **Symbols** command group, we can find a couple of symbols we need to learn to insert.

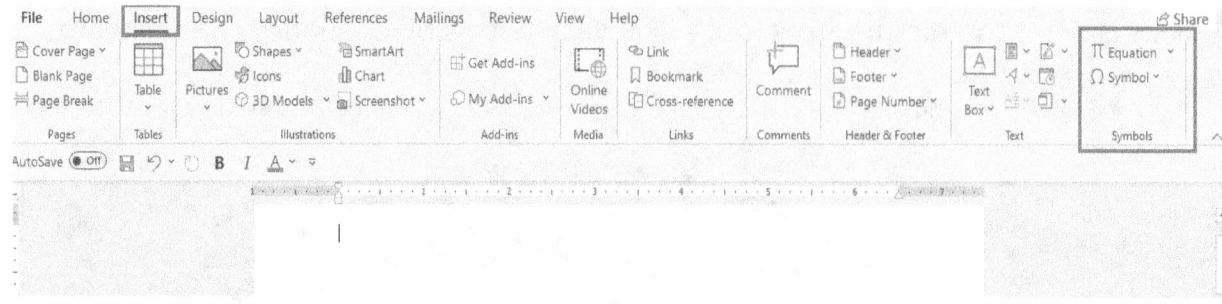

The benefit of using the **Symbols** command group is that you can add several symbols that you cannot find on your regular keyboard. These include **accented letters, foreign language characters, maths symbols, ellipsis, copyright symbols** and various cool symbols.

When you click the **Symbols** dropdown, you first see the more frequently used symbols. If you have used any symbol in the past, it will also be shown here.

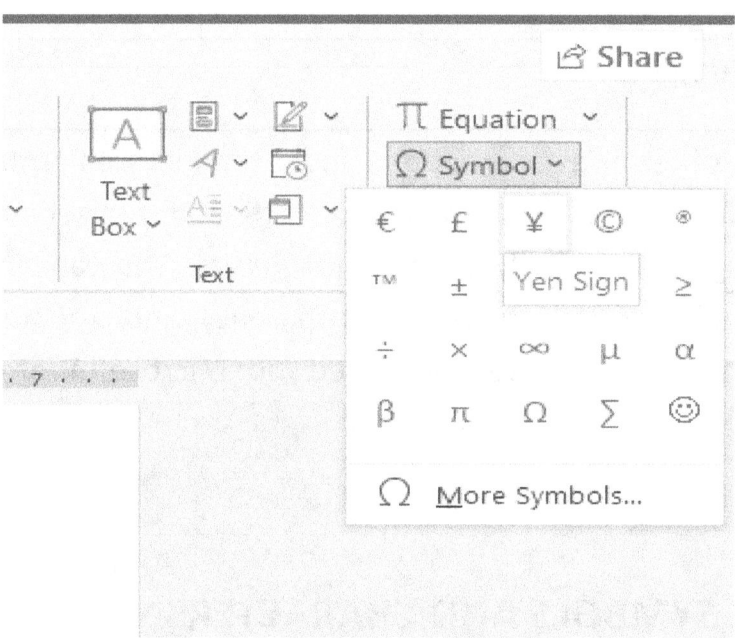

From the picture above, you will find that we have some currency symbols, some Greek symbols, some mathematical symbols, and copyright symbols. These are the most frequent built-in symbols that a majority of Microsoft Word users make use of often.

If you need to insert a given symbol, just go ahead and click it. It will instantly be inserted into your document.

If you want more advanced or specialized symbols, or the whole library of symbols, then click on the **More symbols** option. A new dialog box appears containing the complete library of symbols on Microsoft Word.

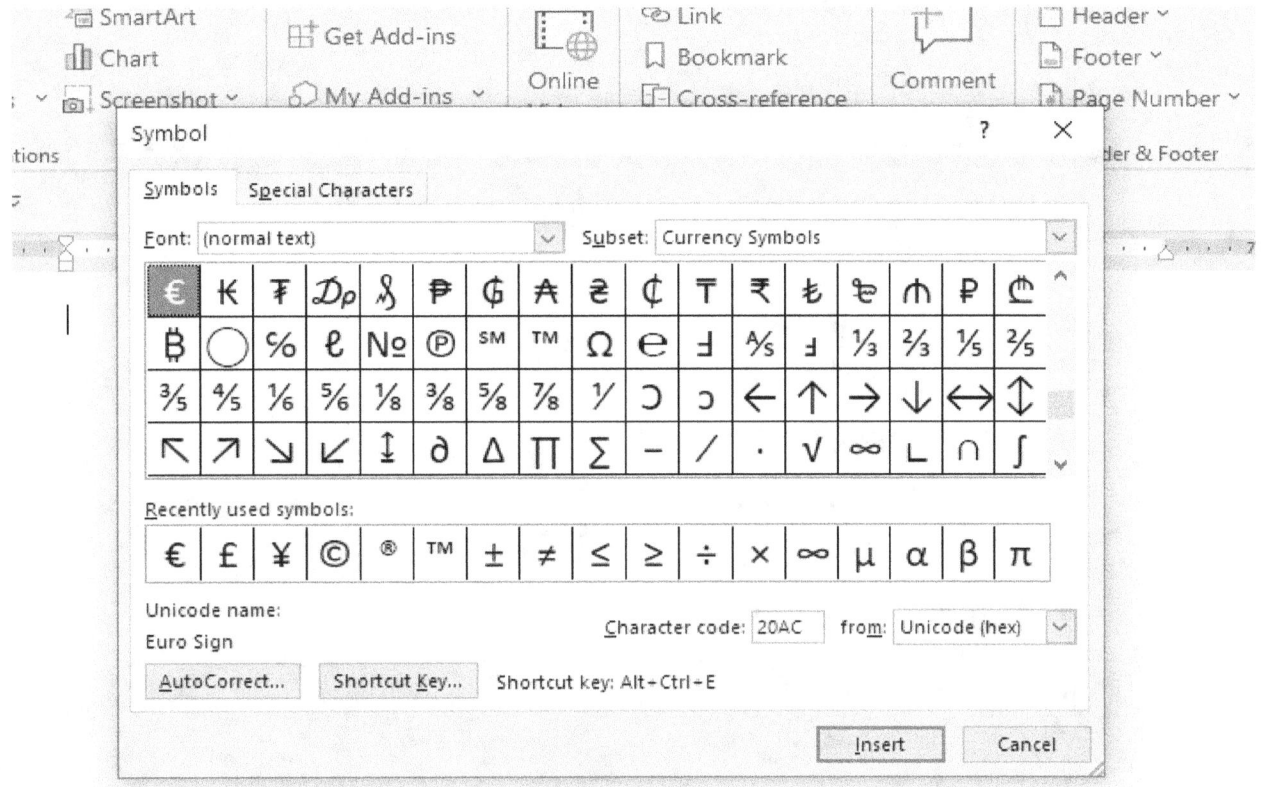

This symbols library is very robust, and you get a lot of different options as well. From this dialog box, you can choose the symbol **font** and get more specialized symbols with the **subset** feature. For any symbol you choose, you will find the Unicode name of the symbol and its character code at the bottom of the dialog box. Also, you can use a shortcut key when you want a quick symbol insertion. For example, the Euro sign is chosen above and its shortcut key is **Alt+Ctrl+E**.

You will notice that there is also a special characters tab. On the special characters tab, you can choose some special characters you need for your documents, like copyright signs, and trademark signs.

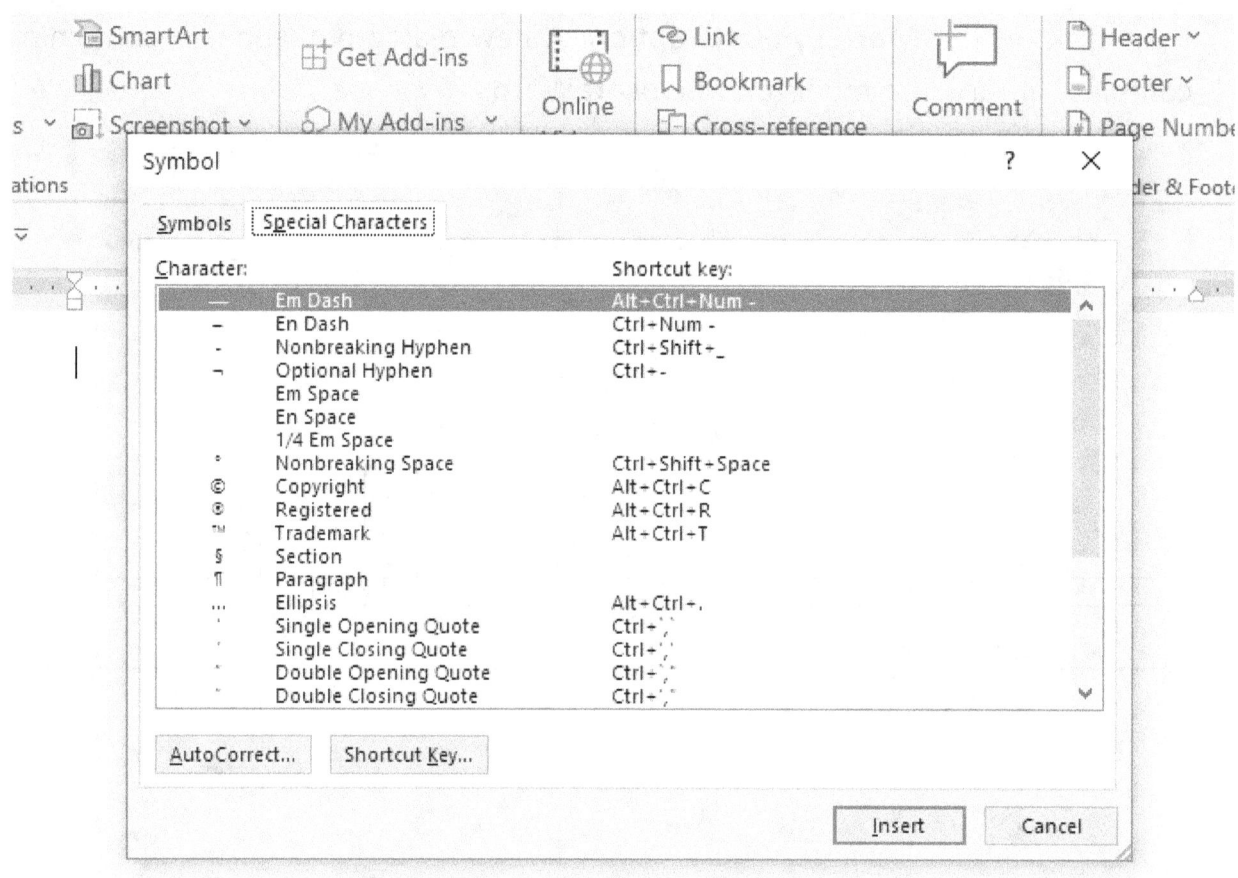

Let's go ahead and add some symbols to a document.

Tip: When you choose a symbol, the subset changes to reflect the chosen symbol subset. Also, some fonts don't have all the symbols. So be mindful when you change fonts for a given symbol.

I will insert a dollar sign, a number sign, and the percent sign in the Algerian font. I will then compare these symbols with their representation in Arial Black font. Notice how the way the symbols are formatted changes.

ALGERIAN FONT = $%#

Arial Black Font = #$%

You can see that the font of your symbol can make a difference in the display on a document.

Practice inserting symbols. Have fun doing so. While doing so, notice the names of a given symbol and whether the symbol is available in the font you prefer. Symbols are one of the coolest stuffs on Microsoft Word.

PART SIX — ADJUSTING PAGE APPEARANCE

Page appearance is a very important topic in Microsoft Word documents. You should plan for how your page will appear before producing a document. Your page appearance will control how you communicate the information in your document.

For the page appearance, we'll discuss two broad topics. First, we'll discuss the **Layout** tab. In this section, we'll specifically concentrate on how to change the orientation of the documentation. We'll also discuss how to select the paper size for a document. After that, we will discuss the **Design** tab. We will look at some of the options in the design tab, such as changing the background color of your entire document, and applying some borders and watermarks as well.

PAGE LAYOUT

To start, let's head over to the **Layout** tab. On the layout tab, there are three command groups. First is the **Page Setup** command group, followed by the **Paragraph** command group, and lastly, the **Arrange** command group.

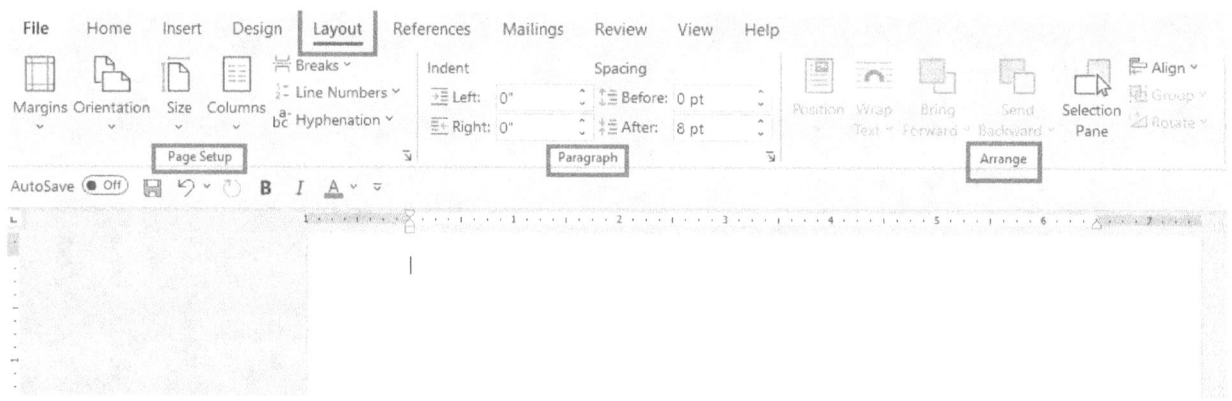

Let's concentrate on the **Page Setup** command group. Here we can see the option to set margins, page orientation, size, and columns.

Let's first concentrate on the margins. These are the blank spaces at the top, the bottom, right and left side of a document. They make a document and page look neat and also professional.

You can select the different measurements for a margin in a document by clicking the **Margins** dropdown in the **Page Setup** command group.

For example, if we start with a page with normal margins with 1 inch on all sides.

After an earthquake, the four lions controlled a forest the size of the United States in the late tenth century. After an earthquake, the four lions controlled a forest the size of the United States in the late tenth century. After an earthquake, the four lions controlled a forest the size of the United States in the late tenth century. After an earthquake, the four lions controlled a forest the size of the United States in the late tenth century.

After an earthquake, the four lions controlled a forest the size of the United States in the late tenth century. After an earthquake, the four lions controlled a forest the size of the United States in the late tenth century. After an earthquake, the four lions controlled a forest the size of the United States in the late tenth century. After an earthquake, the four lions controlled a forest the size of the United States in the late tenth century.

After an earthquake, the four lions controlled a forest the size of the United States in the late tenth century. After an earthquake, the four lions controlled a forest the size of the United States in the late tenth century. After an earthquake, the four lions controlled a forest the size of the United States in the late tenth century. After an earthquake, the four lions controlled a forest the size of the United States in the late tenth century.

After an earthquake, the four lions controlled a forest the size of the United States in the late tenth century. After an earthquake, the four lions controlled a forest the size of the United States in the late tenth century. After an earthquake, the four lions controlled a forest the size of the United States in the late tenth century. After an earthquake, the four lions controlled a forest the size of the United States in

We could make the margins bigger and increase the number of pages by increasing the margins on the left and right sides. For this, we need to choose the wide margins option with the left and right-side margins being 2 inches.

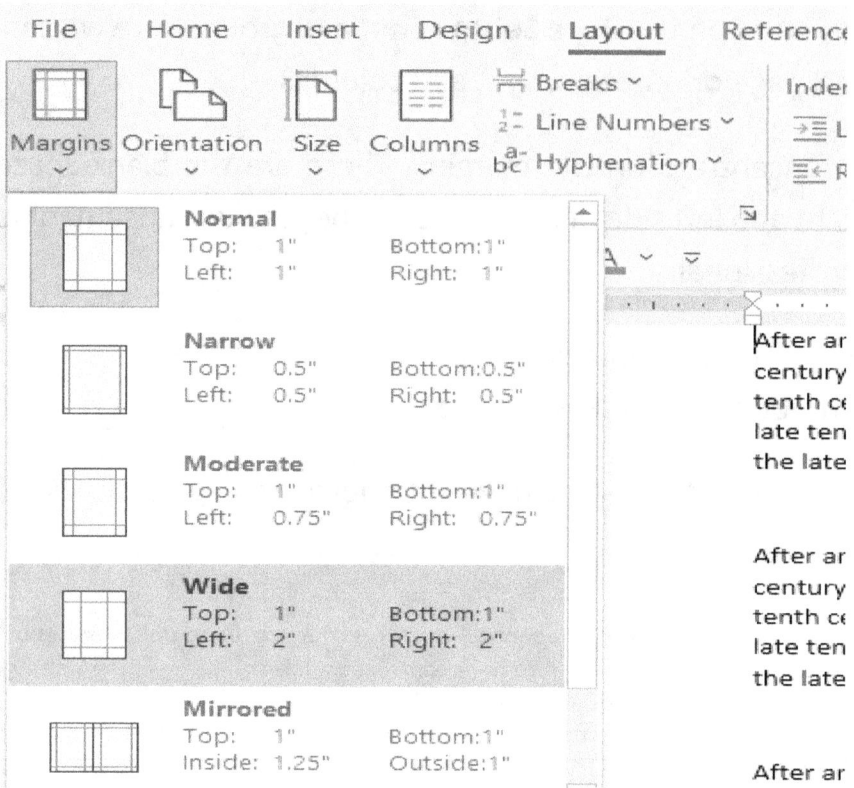

After applying this margin, our page layout will have wider left and right margins. Therefore, the pages will become more, and the space for the text will become less.

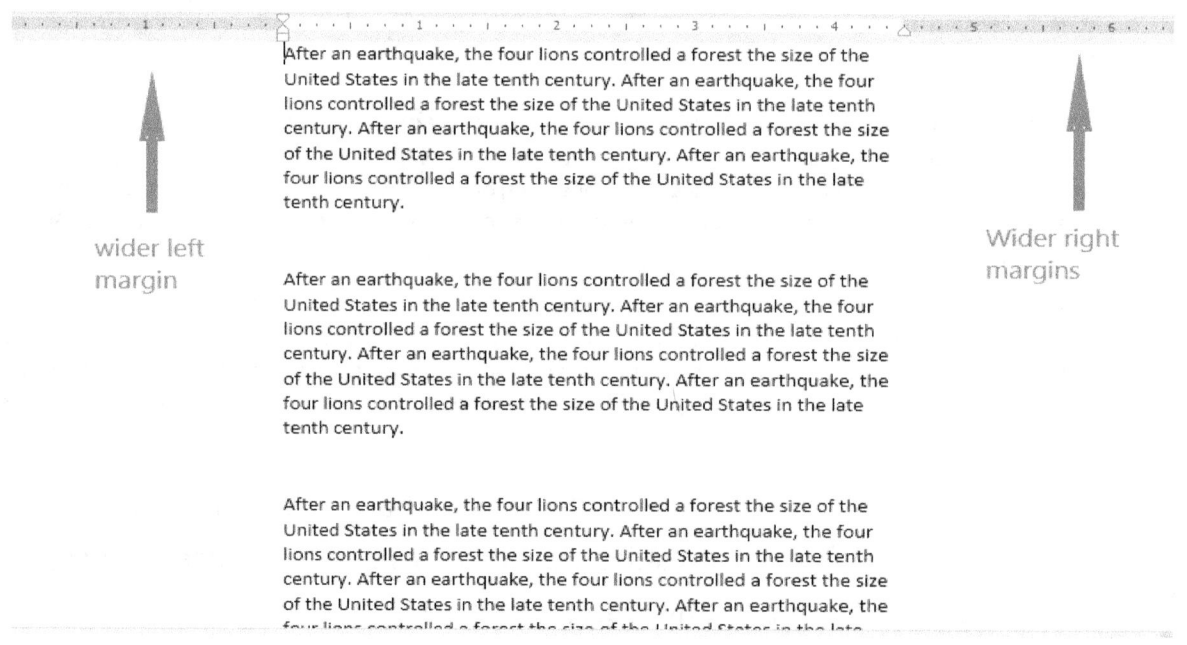

We could also decrease the left and right margins. An option for doing this is the narrow margins option.

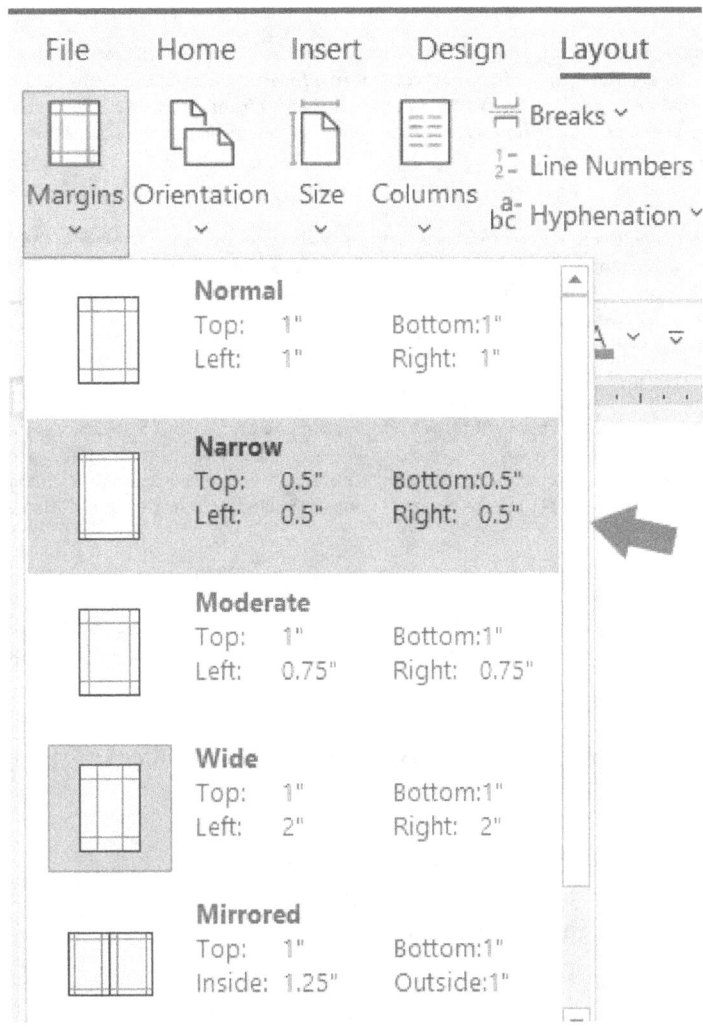

Experiment with these options and see what effect they will give on your documents.

Page Orientation

Another way we could enhance the layout of our documents and pages is through the **orientation** command. Orientation affects the spacing and appearance of text. In Microsoft Word, we have two orientation types: **Portrait** and **Landscape**. Portrait is the default. Portrait is the vertical mode while the landscape is the horizontal mode.

This is what the Portrait or vertical mode looks like. It is the default.

After an earthquake, the four lions controlled a forest the size of the United States in the late tenth century. After an earthquake, the four lions controlled a forest the size of the United States in the late tenth century. After an earthquake, the four lions controlled a forest the size of the United States in the late tenth century. After an earthquake, the four lions controlled a forest the size of the United States in the late tenth century.

After an earthquake, the four lions controlled a forest the size of the United States in the late tenth century. After an earthquake, the four lions controlled a forest the size of the United States in the late tenth century. After an earthquake, the four lions controlled a forest the size of the United States in the late tenth century. After an earthquake, the four lions controlled a forest the size of the United States in the late tenth century.

After an earthquake, the four lions controlled a forest the size of the United States in the late tenth century. After an earthquake, the four lions controlled a forest the size of the United States in the late tenth century. After an earthquake, the four lions controlled a forest the size of the United States in the late tenth century. After an earthquake, the four lions controlled a forest the size of the United States in the late tenth century.

After an earthquake, the four lions controlled a forest the size of the United States in the late tenth century. After an earthquake, the four lions controlled a forest the size of the United States in the late tenth century. After an earthquake, the four lions controlled a forest the size of the United States in

Compare it to the landscape or horizontal mode. Notice how wider the landscape mode is.

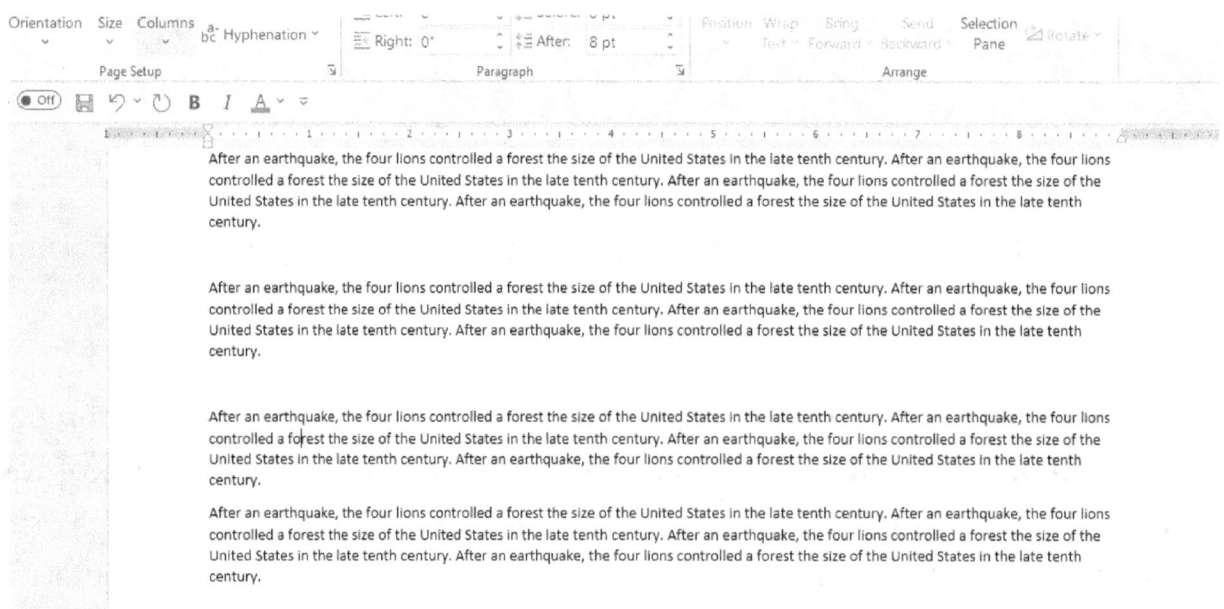

People usually use the landscape mode when they want a wider document because the elements in the document such as images and tables need more space. They are good for making brochures.

Page Size

Another feature that affects a page's layout is the **Size** command. With the size command, you can change the size of the pages in your document. The default is the letter size which is 8.5 inches by 11 inches. You could find the A4 size more convenient for your printing needs because most papers are in A4 size.

Finally, another feature of page layout we would like to practice on is the **Columns** command. This command allows you to split a page into more than one column. This gives your pages a newspaper or magazine layout. This command is useful when you want to create documents like brochures, newsletters, or any multi-column publication.

We will now split our document's pages into two columns per page. Here is what it looks like.

After an earthquake, the four lions controlled a forest the size of the United States in the late tenth century. After an earthquake, the four lions controlled a forest the size of the United States in the late tenth century. After an earthquake, the four lions controlled a forest the size of the United States in the late tenth century. After an earthquake, the four lions controlled a forest the size of the United States in the late tenth century. After an earthquake, the four lions controlled a forest the size of the United States in the late tenth century.

After an earthquake, the four lions controlled a forest the size of the United States in the late tenth century. After an earthquake, the four lions controlled a forest the size of the United States in the late tenth century. After an earthquake, the four lions controlled a forest the size of the United States in the late tenth century. After an earthquake, the four lions controlled a forest the size of the United States in the late tenth century. After an earthquake, the four lions controlled a forest the size of the United States in the late tenth century.

After an earthquake, the four lions controlled a forest the size of the United States in the late tenth century. After an earthquake, the four lions controlled a forest the size of the United States in the late tenth century. After an earthquake, the four lions controlled a forest the size of the United States in the late tenth century. After an earthquake, the four lions controlled a forest the size of the United States in the late tenth century.

After an earthquake, the four lions controlled a forest the size of the United States in the late tenth century. After an earthquake, the four lions controlled a forest the size of the United States in the late tenth century. After an earthquake, the four lions controlled a forest the size of the United States in the late tenth century. After an earthquake, the four lions controlled a forest the size of the United States in the late tenth century.

You can try out other columns like three, four, or even more columns with this command.

PAGE DESIGN

Now let's go on to the **Design** tab. For this guide, we will be concentrating on the **Page Background** command group.

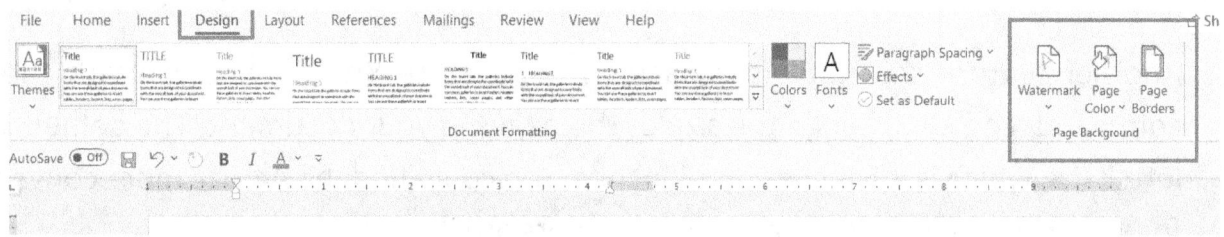

Adding Borders

The first item we will consider in that group is the **Page Borders**. Page borders provide a frame around the text. This enhances the visual appeal of each page to readers. They also add a decorative touch to pages. With page borders, you can highlight different sections of a document.

When you click on the **Page Borders** command, you get a dialog box that asks you to pick the **style**, **color**, **width**, and **art** of the borders. You could apply the chosen borders to the whole document or sections of the document. You chose what you want.

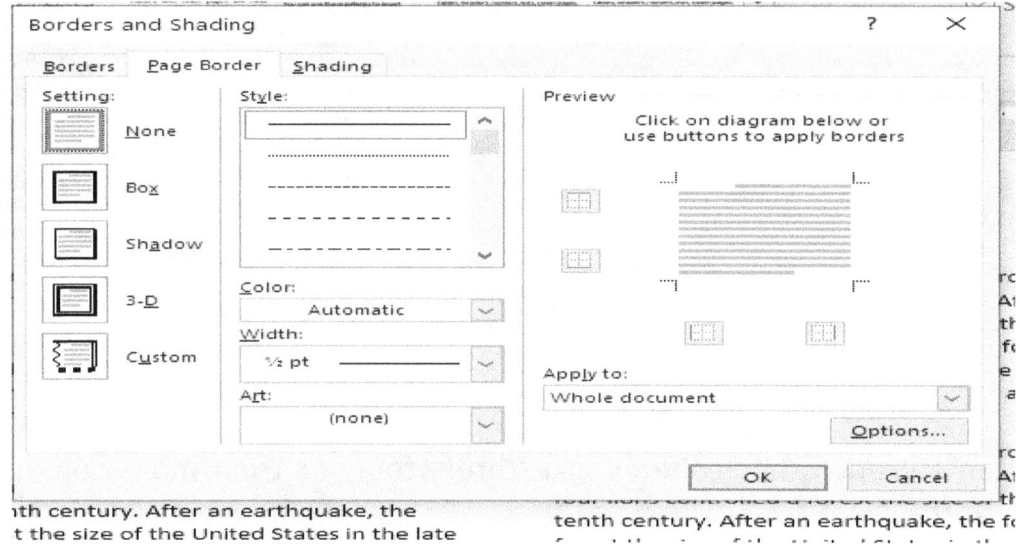

th century. After an earthquake, the
t the size of the United States in the late

tenth century. After an earthquake, the fo

Let's pick some options for page borders and apply these options to the whole document. We will then look at the effect it gives on the document.

For this exercise, we will choose a style of double lines, with blue color with a width of 28 points. Then, we will choose an art style for the borders.

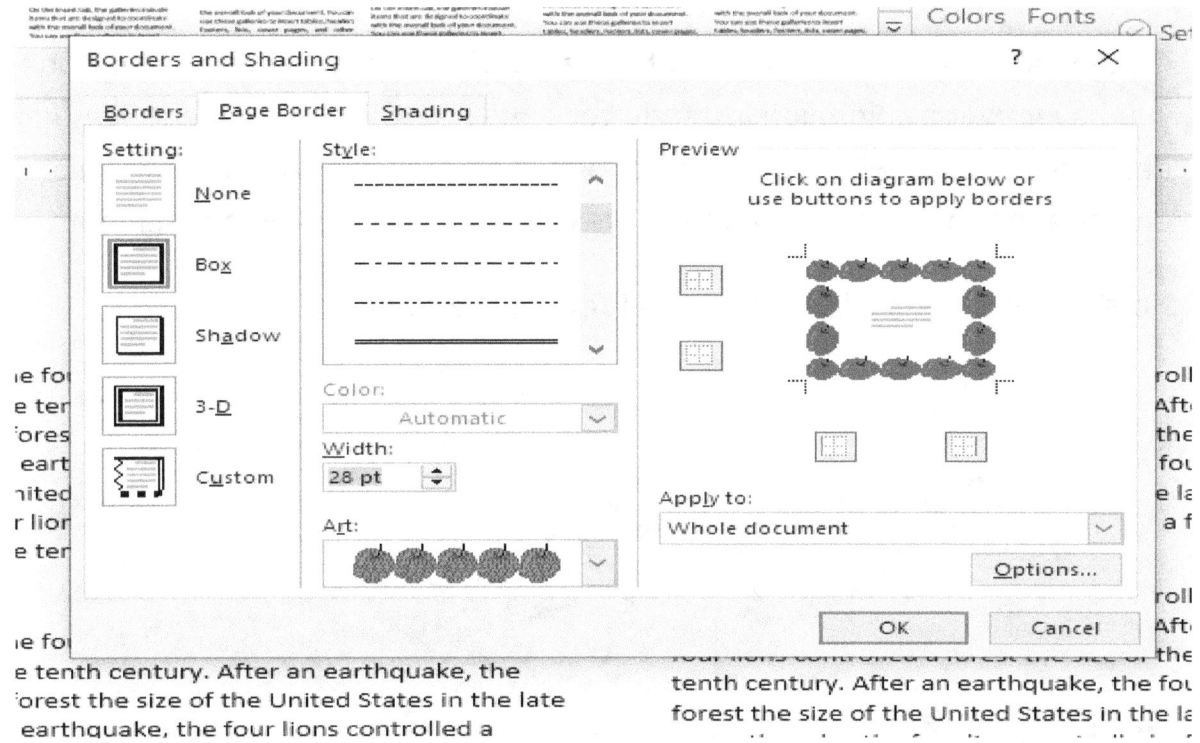

Here is what the page borders look like.

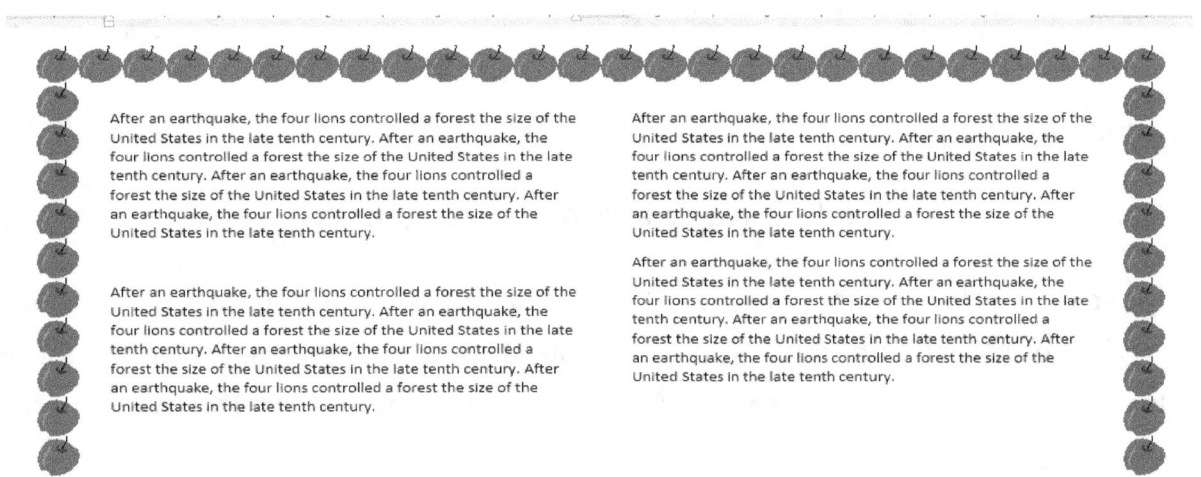

You must agree that page borders enhance the document's visual appeal and pages.

Adding Page Color

The next feature that deals with page design are page color. It is used to change the color of a page. This enhances the beauty of the page.

On the **Page Color** dropdown, you have a lot of theme colors to choose from. When you hover over a color, you instantly get a preview of the document. This helps the designer to know what colors to choose. A rule of thumb is choosing colors that enhance the contrast between the page color and the document's elements.

Here, I have chosen a light blue tone for the page color.

After an earthquake, the four lions controlled a forest the size of the United States in the late tenth century. After an earthquake, the four lions controlled a forest the size of the United States in the late tenth century. After an earthquake, the four lions controlled a forest the size of the United States in the late tenth century. After an earthquake, the four lions controlled a forest the size of the United States in the late tenth century.

tenth century. After an earthquake, the four lions controlled a forest the size of the United States in the late tenth century. After an earthquake, the four lions controlled a forest the size of the United States in the late tenth century.

After an earthquake, the four lions controlled a forest the size of the United States in the late tenth century. After an earthquake, the

Adding Watermarks

Finally, some watermarks could be added to a document or page.

Most often, watermarks are used to set the status of a document. The document might be official, confidential, or a sample. With the watermark, we let the reader know the document's purpose. A logo can also be set as the watermark for a document.

When you click the **Watermarks** command under the **Page Background** command group, you get a dialog box for watermarks classified according to categories or sections. You could also specify a custom watermark which could be your company logo.

Let's classify our document as confidential with a watermark.

After an earthquake, the four lions controlled a forest the size of the United States in the late tenth century. After an earthquake, the four lions controlled a forest the size of the United States in the late tenth century. After an earthquake, the four lions controlled a forest the size of the United States in the late tenth century. After an earthquake, the four lions controlled a forest the size of the United States in the late tenth century.

tenth century. After an earthquake, the four lions controlled a forest the size of the United States in the late tenth century. After an earthquake, the four lions controlled a forest the size of the United States in the late tenth century.

After an earthquake, the four lions controlled a forest the size of the

You can see the **Confidential** watermark embedded in the document diagonally. There are other position options for the watermark, like displaying it horizontally.

We have covered a lot of ground in page layout and design. I want you to go ahead and try out these new concepts on your own. Create a document and give it various page layouts. Then, design it using the different **Page Background** command group commands outlined above.

HEADERS AND FOOTERS

At the top of each page, there is a space where you can insert a header. Also, at the bottom, there is a space for inserting a footer.

We use headers and footers to add information to a page. This information could be page numbers, dates, and document titles at the top or bottom of each page of a document. Many professionals use it to make their document design consistent across all pages by adding a logo at the top. One advantage of headers and footers is that it makes it easier for readers to navigate the document. It can also provide a reference to elements in the document.

The option to add headers and footers is on the **Insert** tab at the **Header & Footer** command group.

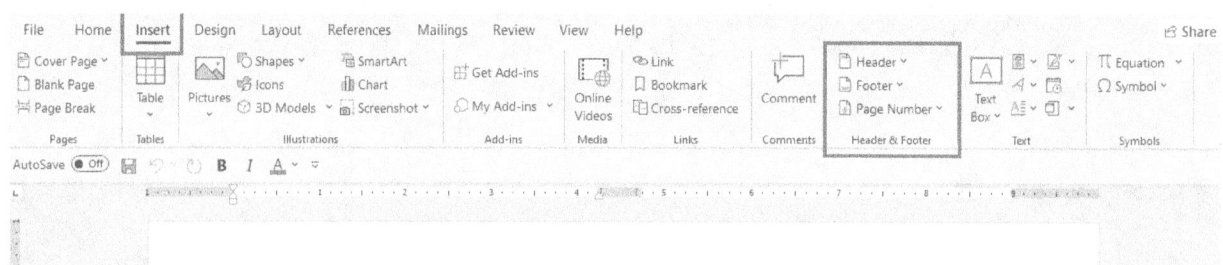

To insert a header, click on the **Header** command dropdown, and some options to insert headers appear. It could be a blank header, three columns, or an Austin header. Let's start with a blank header.

Immediately, a space appears at the top of the page with a contextual menu called **Header & Footer**. The contextual menu helps you with manipulating the information you want to put into the header. Using the contextual menu, we can add dates and time information, our textual information, or even pictures like company logos. We can also position the information. After we are done adding information and executing it, the command to close the contextual menu for headers and footers is at the far right...

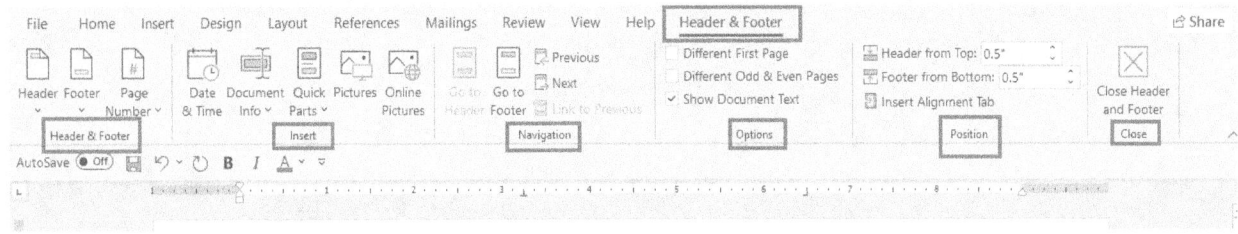

I will add some information to the header here. I will just put **Microsoft Word 2021** and close the contextual menu. You will notice that at the top of the page, this information now appears after I close the contextual menu.

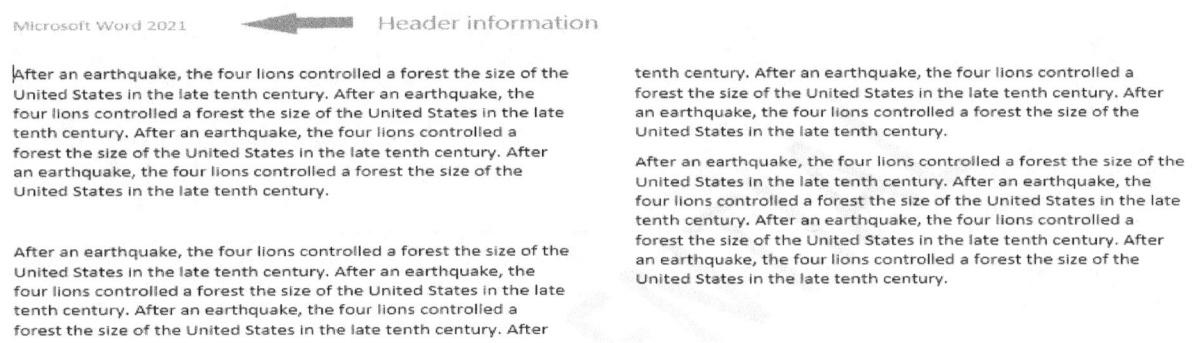

We can add a footer the same way we added headers above. Note that footers are at the bottom of the page.

Page Number

Another feature you will most likely need in a document is a page number. Page numbers are part of the headers and footers because you can add a page number at the top or bottom of a page.

To insert a page number, on the **Header & Footer** command group, click **Page Number**. A box appears with options for positioning the page number to be inserted or removing it.

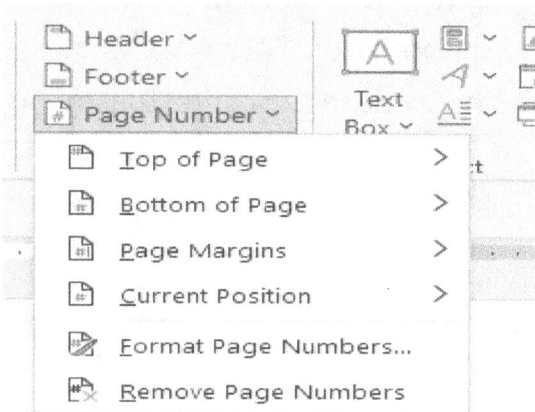

We'll insert a page number at the top of the page. Another box appears where you can specify the actual positioning of the page numbers. We'll choose the third option, **Plain Number 3**, that is, to position it on the right side.

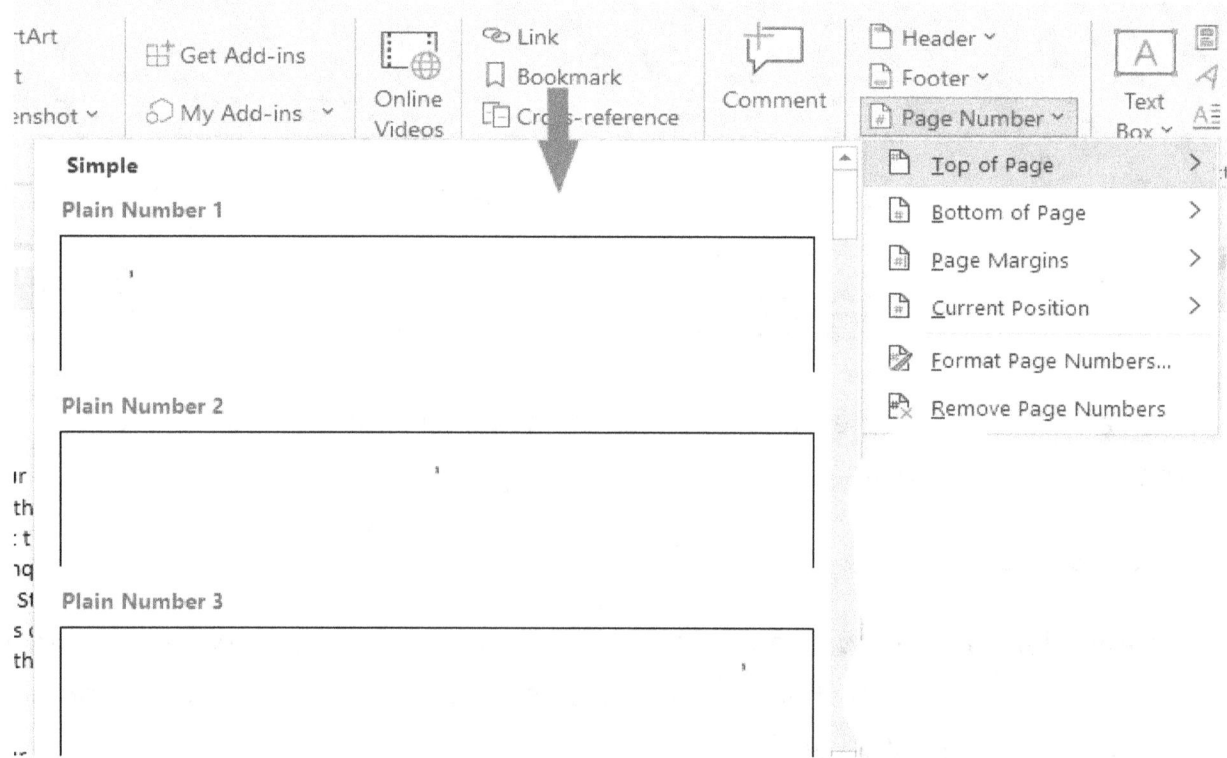

A contextual menu for **Header & Footer** now appears. It is the same contextual menu as we saw for inserting headers and footers. We can use this contextual menu to do more formatting on the page number. But for now, we are happy as it is and we'll close the contextual menu.

Page
Number 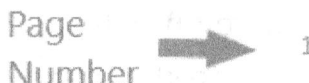 1

tenth century. After an earthquake, the four lions controlled a forest the size of the United States in the late tenth century. After an earthquake, the four lions controlled a forest the size of the United States in the late tenth century.

After an earthquake, the four lions controlled a forest the size of the United States in the late tenth century. After an earthquake, the four lions controlled a forest the size of the United States in the late tenth century. After an earthquake, the four lions controlled a forest the size of the United States in the late tenth century. After an earthquake, the four lions controlled a forest the size of the

At this point, I will encourage you to start practicing inserting headers and footers, including page numbers.

It is essential that you proofread your document and also carry out other reviews before publishing it to the world. This chapter will cover techniques to use with Microsoft Word.

PROOFING AND REVIEWING YOUR DOCUMENT

The review tab in Microsoft Word is helpful in many ways in preparing your document. With it you can:

- Improve the grammar and spelling of your document.
- Format your document
- Make sure your document is error-free
- Track changes in a document with colleagues and collaborators
- Check your document for accessibility

Proofing

You can find the proofing and review features on the Review tab.

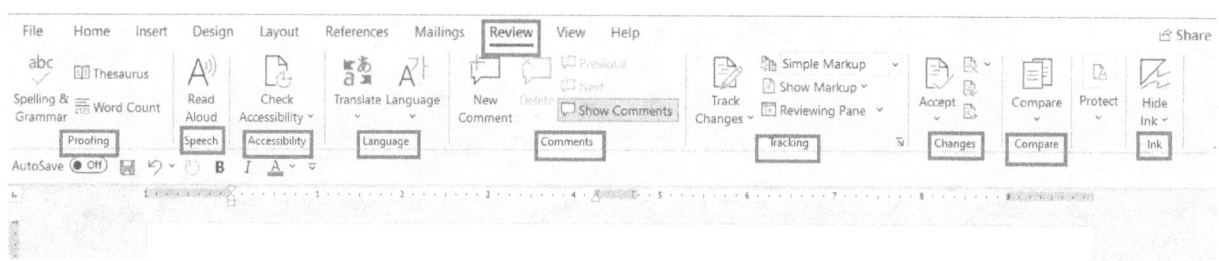

On the **Proofing** command group, you can find that we have three commands there: **Spelling & Grammar, Thesaurus, and Word Count**.

The **Spelling & Grammar** command helps you to spell-check your document for errors. Whenever you have finished typing your text, clicking on this command will do a spell-check on your document. When it finds a word with wrong spelling, it is underlined in red ink.

The **Thesaurus** feature helps you to rephrase your words and sentences. Maybe you are at a loss for how to change your words and you don't want to use the same word, Microsoft Word Thesaurus feature will give you optional words that will be used for this. When you click on the Thesaurus command, a text box appears to the right of the document with suggested words.

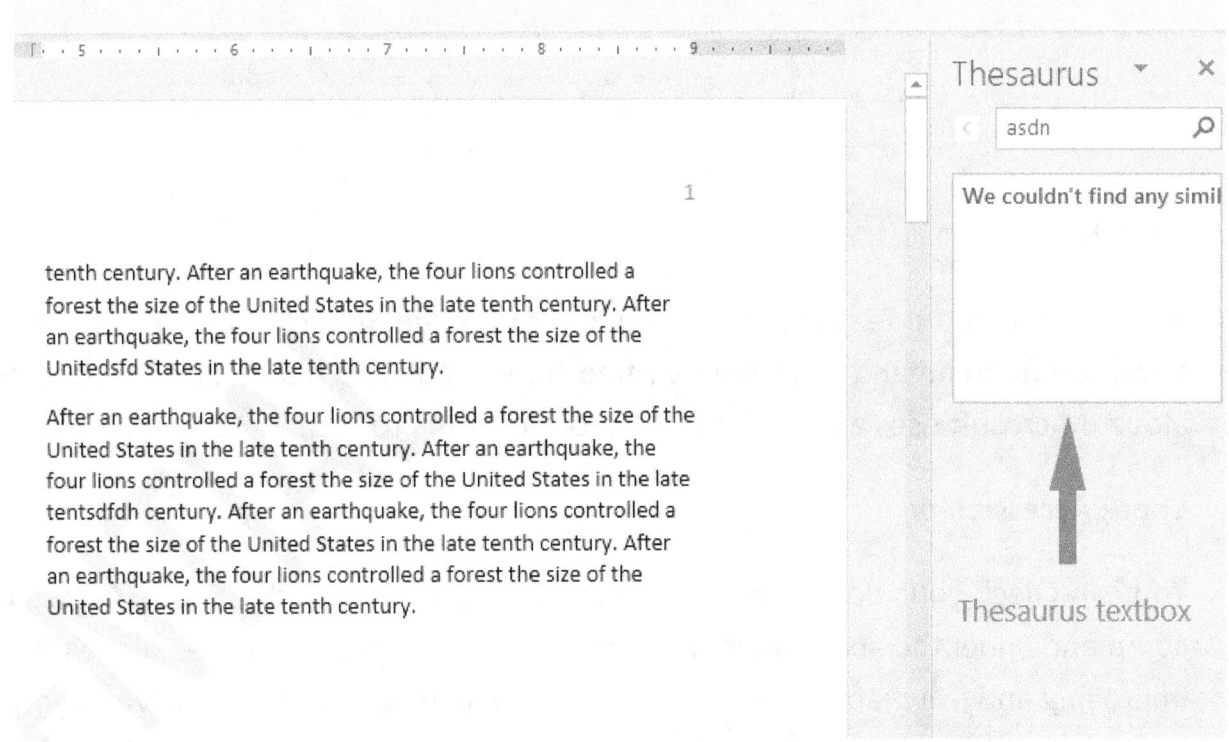

Then, the **Word Count** command gives you information on how many words are in your document. Many writers find this useful because they are often tasked with writing within a given number of words. On clicking this command, a dialog box appears that tells you how many pages your document has, the number of words, characters, and paragraphs. You can see from the image below that my document has 363 words and 3 pages.

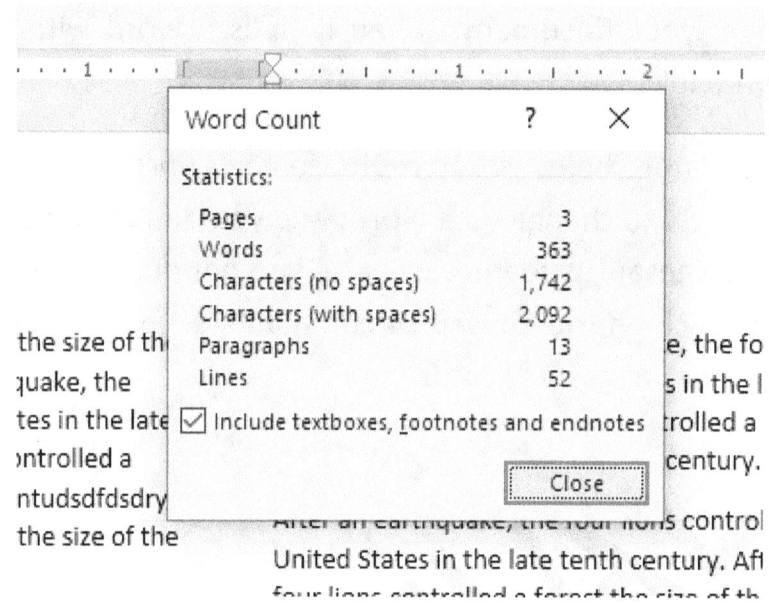

Speech

Another wonderful feature on the **Review** tab is the **Speech** command group. The **Read Aloud** command that you can find here reads the words on your document aloud. Microsoft uses a male voice to read the words to you.

Check Accessibility

You can check your document for accessibility issues using the **Check Accessibility** command under the **accessibility** command group. This tool provides suggestions for improving and fixing any accessibility issues found in your document. When you click the **Check Accessibility** dropdown menu, it gives you options for checking accessibility, adding Alt Text to images, having a Navigation pane in your document, and also checking for ease of access.

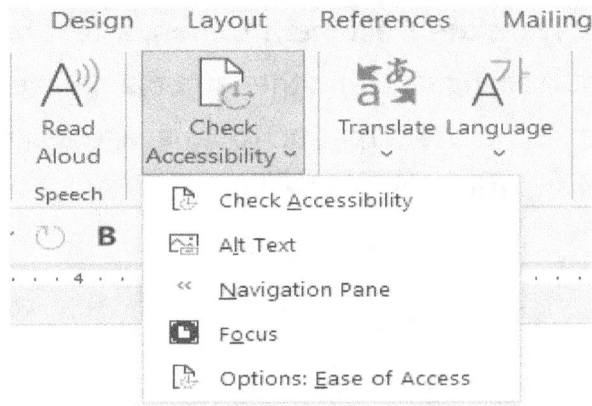

The accessibility tools are helpful if you want your documents to be available to people with disabilities or if it has to be viewed on a screen reader.

Language

You have two commands on the **Language** command group in the review tab: **Translate** and **Language**. The **Translate** command enables you to translate content in your document into another language. The **Language** command enables you to change or choose the language you want your proofing tools to use. The default is English.

When you click on the Translate command dropdown menu, it gives you two options: translating a selection of the document or the whole document. Let's translate the whole document.

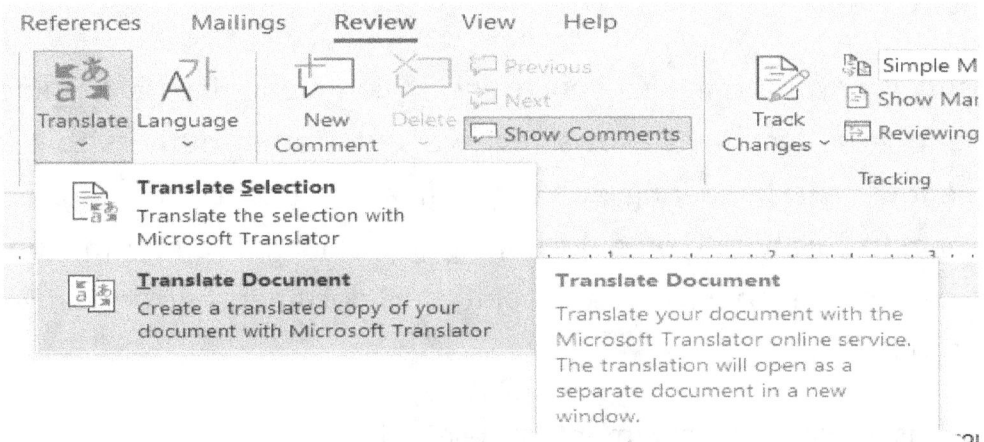

When you click the **Translate Document** option, a text box appears on the side for you to select the source language and the target language. For this, we will leave the source as Auto-detect and the target or **To** language as French. Then, we'll click the **Translator** for the translation task to begin.

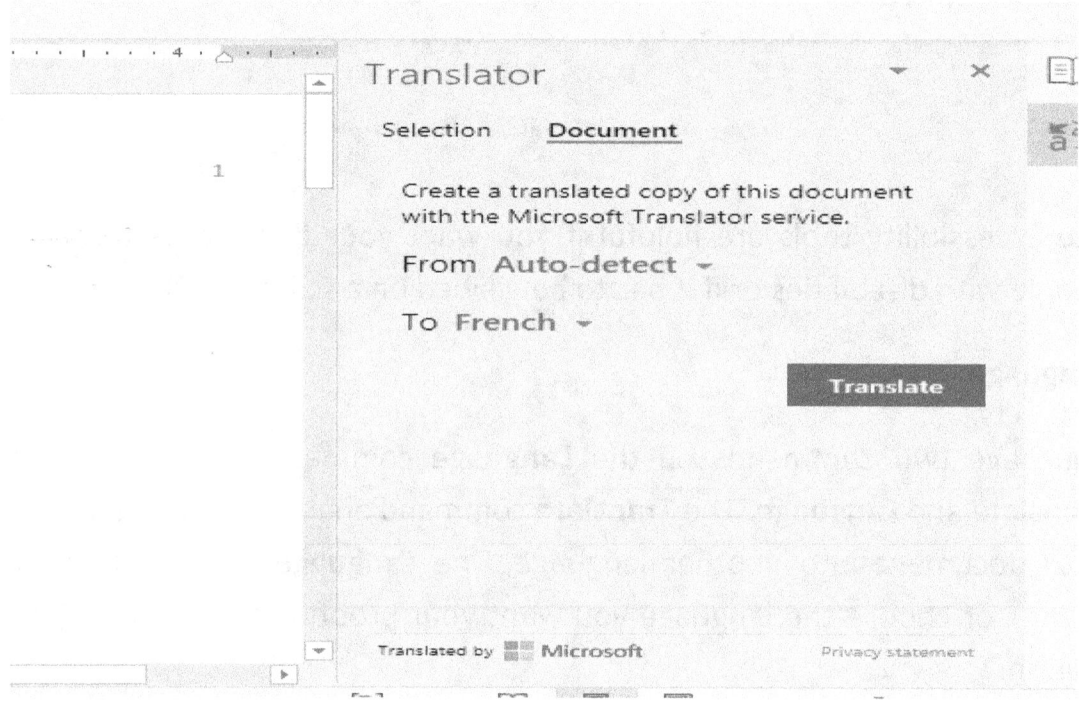

After the translation is complete, the translated document will open in a separate window.

Comment

Microsoft Word also enables you to insert comments into a document. Inserting comments in a document allows reviewers and other authors to add notes to a document without tampering with the original document. This feature makes it easy for a team to collaborate on a document or provide more information and context. Many teams use comments to point out document errors or areas needing modification.

You can insert, change a comment, or delete it.

To insert a comment, select the text that has to be commented on. Then click **New Comment** on the **Review** tab. A textbox appears with your name where you can insert the comment. In the image above, I selected a phrase with an incorrect word and inserted a comment on it.

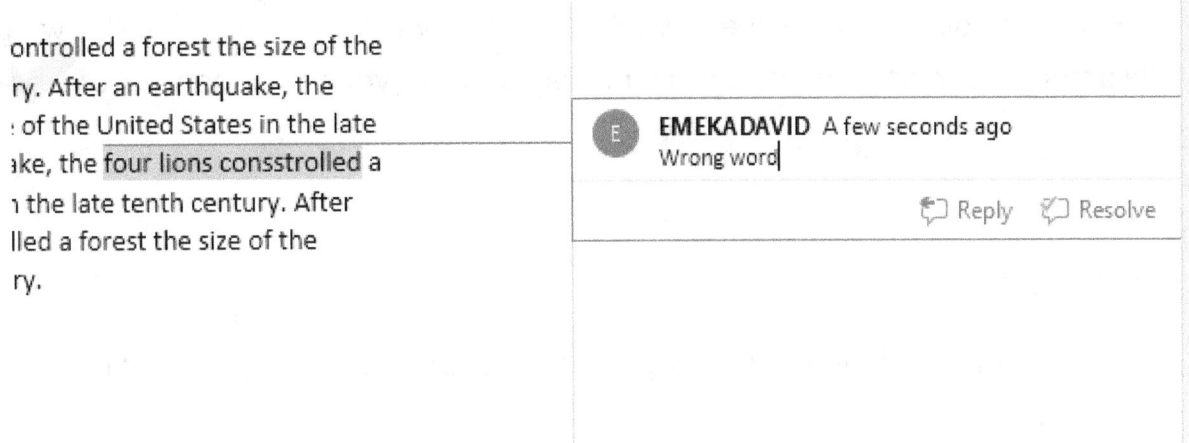

You can also reply to a comment. You can see the reply button in the image above. Just click on the comment and when the textbox appears, click on **Reply** and then insert your reply.

One can also delete a comment or all the comments in a document. Just click the dropdown menu on the **Delete** comment command to do this. Then choose the option you want.

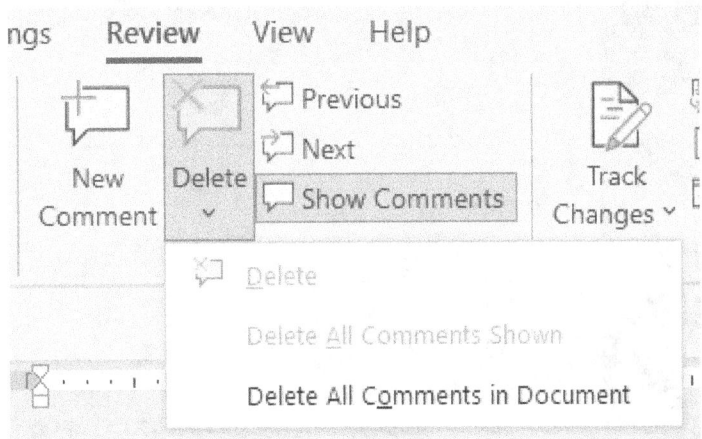

There are a lot of other things you can do to prepare your document. You can track changes and accept or reject changes. You can also compare two documents together to find out the similarities and differences.

I encourage you to explore the possibilities you have for proofing and reviewing your document. Your effort now goes a long way to make your documents professional.

PRINTING

In this section, we'll discuss printing documents and converting a word document to other file formats.

To access the printing function, just click on the **File** Menu, and then the start screen will appear immediately. Then click on **Print**.

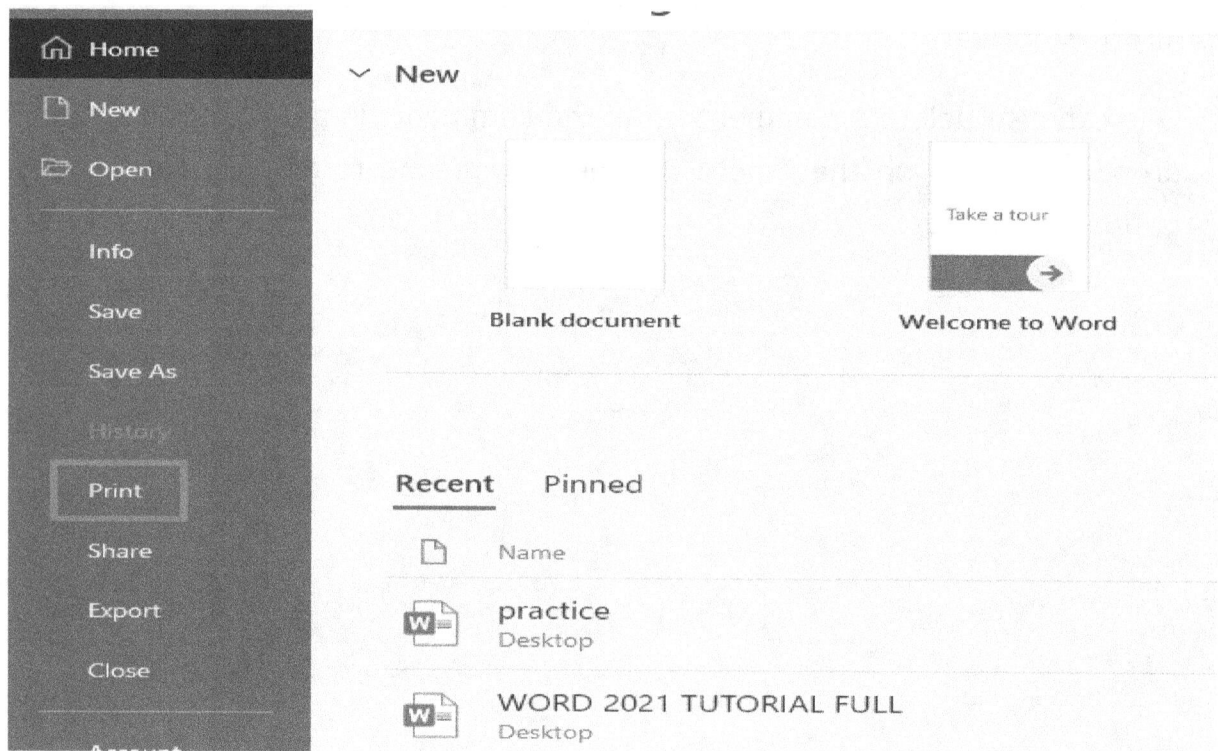

The **print** dialog box will immediately appear. On the print dialog box, you will find the printers you have installed on your computer and the print setting. For this demonstration, we will assume there is no printer on the computer. So, we will choose, for a printer, the **Microsoft Print to PDF** option. We will leave the settings as they are.

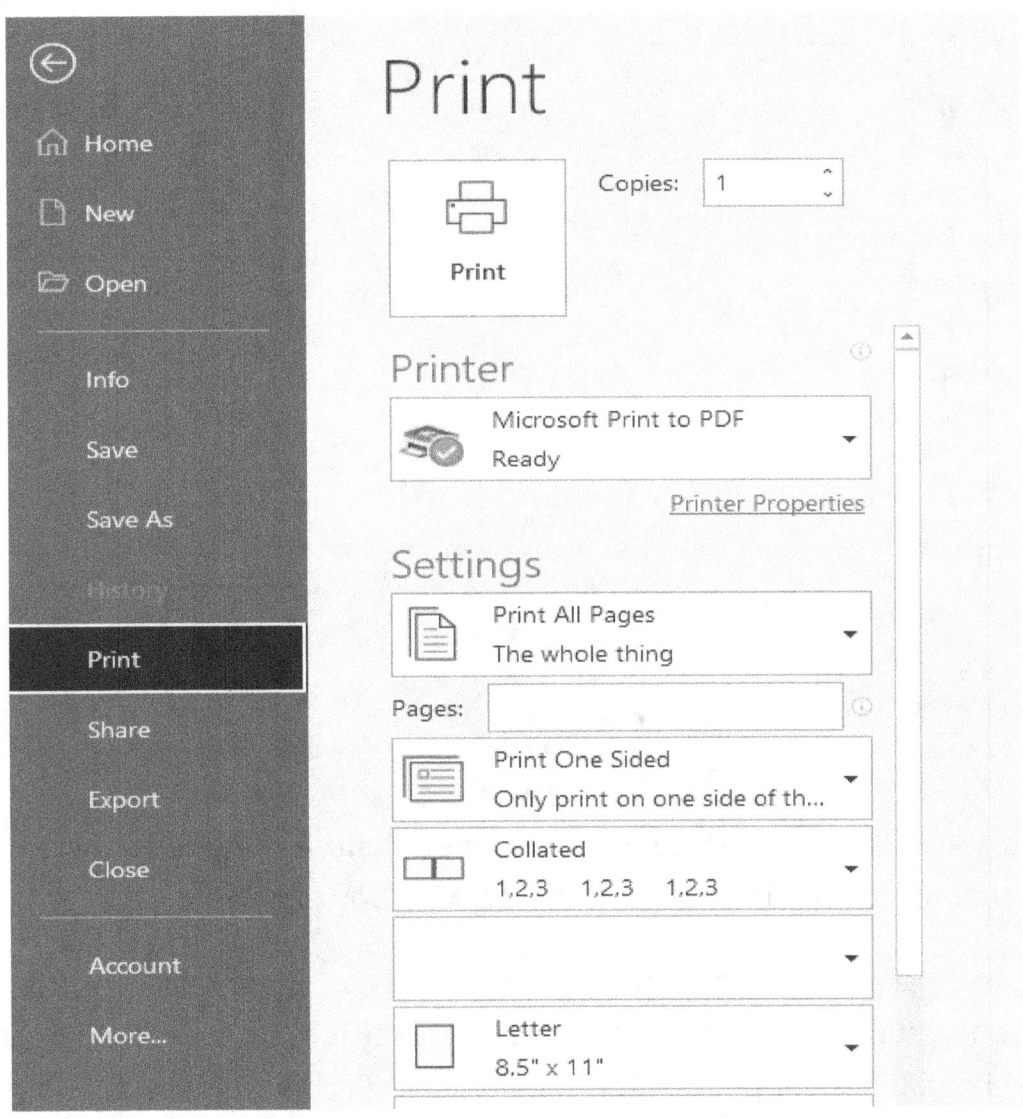

When you are satisfied with the chosen printer and settings, just click on the Print button, and your document will immediately be sent to the chosen printer. In this case, we will have a PDF document. I specified to print just 1 copy and before it printed it out to PDF, it prompted me to save the file with a file name in the **Save Print Output As** dialog box.

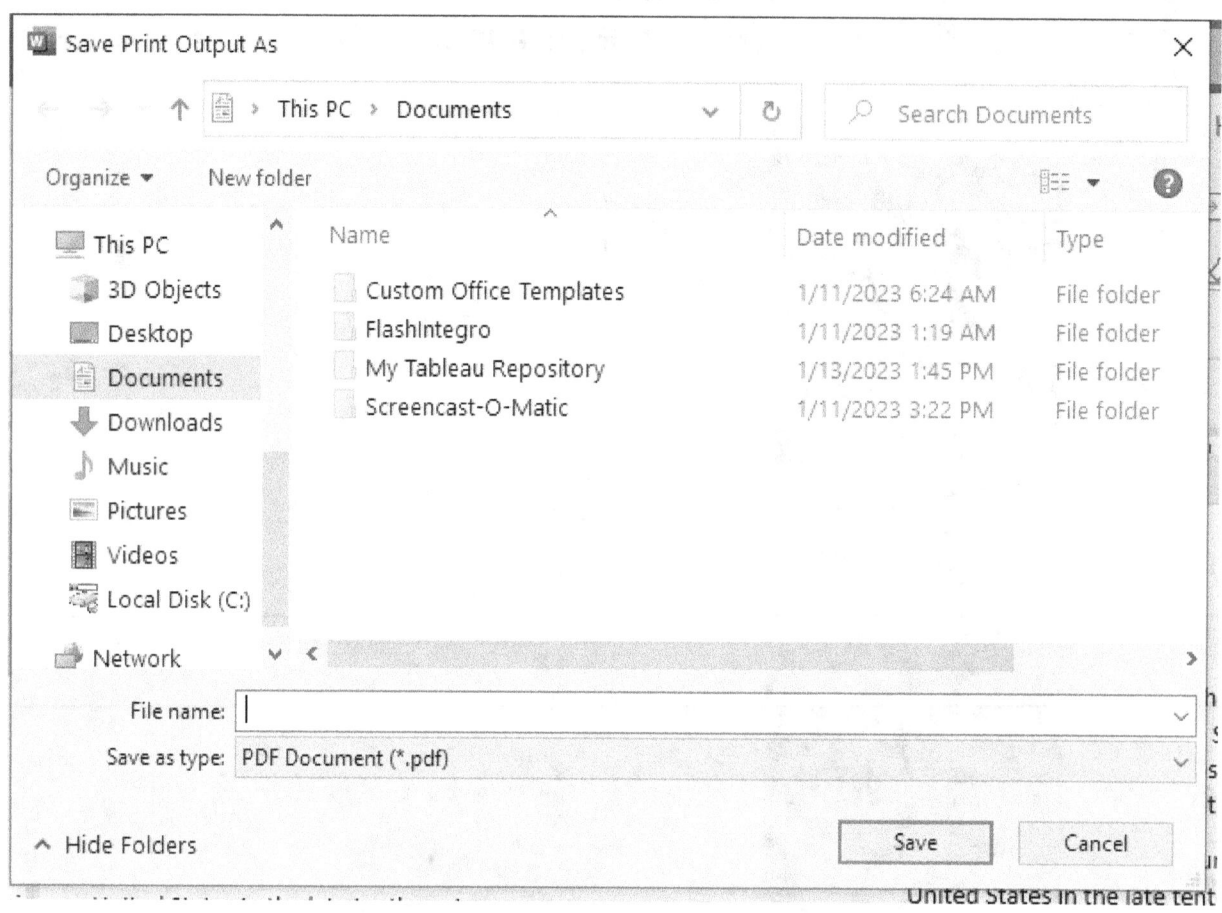

It is a good practice to review your document before printing so that you will make sure that what the printer outputs will be what you expected.

Also, to get a good printer output, it is essential you understand the print settings. In the print settings page, the first option you will see is the option to choose the number of copies you want to print. This is the number of copies for a page.

Next is the option to select the printer you will use. You can choose software printers like printing as a PDF we discussed above, printing to Fax, or a hardware physical printer. While choosing a printer, you can use the **Printer Properties** link to choose what orientation the document should appear. The options are **Landscape** or **Portrait**. Landscape is wider than Portrait.

Next is the **Print All Pages** option, where you specify whether all the pages will be printed or just some chosen pages. You could tell Microsoft Word to print only odd pages or only even pages. The options can be found on the dropdown menu.

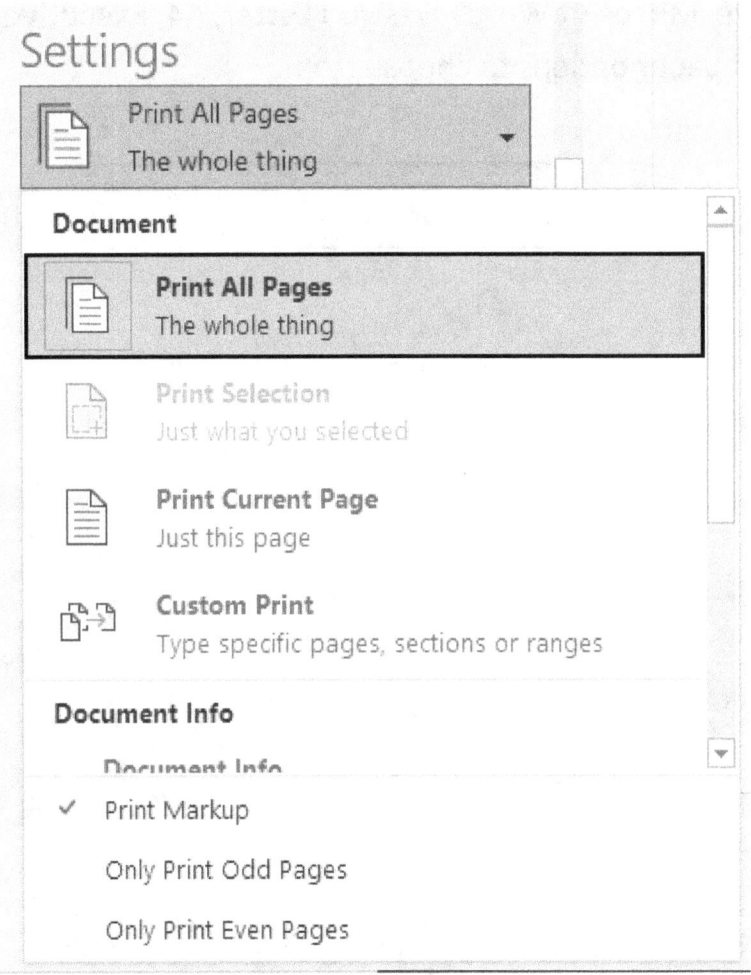

Next is the **Print One Sided** option, where you can specify to print only one side or both sides of the document.

Next is the **Collated** option. For collated, we want to print the pages in a specific order. For example, you want to print 2 copies of each page in a document. For collated, if the document is 5 pages, it will print pages 1 to 5 first, and then in a second run, it will print pages 1 to 5. But for uncollated, it will print page 1 twice, page 2 twice, until you get to page 5 which is printed twice.

Then in the **Lette**r option, you have to choose the type of paper. This has already been covered under the page appearance part. But you can still choose here to change it at the last minute. Microsoft Word gives you **Letter, A4, Executive, Tabloid, A3, A5,** and other types of paper options to choose from.

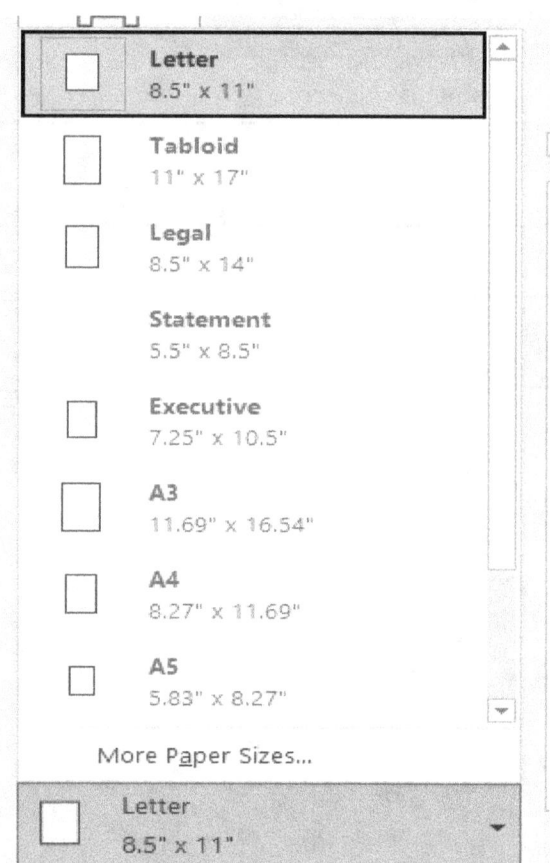

Finally, you have the option to align the margins and choose the number of pages you want per sheet. The default is one page per sheet.

The nice thing about Microsoft Word is that while you make these settings changes, you will get a nice preview page to the right. The preview page will show you how your document will appear in the printed copy. You also have a navigation button at the bottom where you can scroll through the pages.

SHARING YOUR DOCUMENT

Another thing we can do with our document is to share the document. The **Share** button is just under the **Print** button on the start screen.

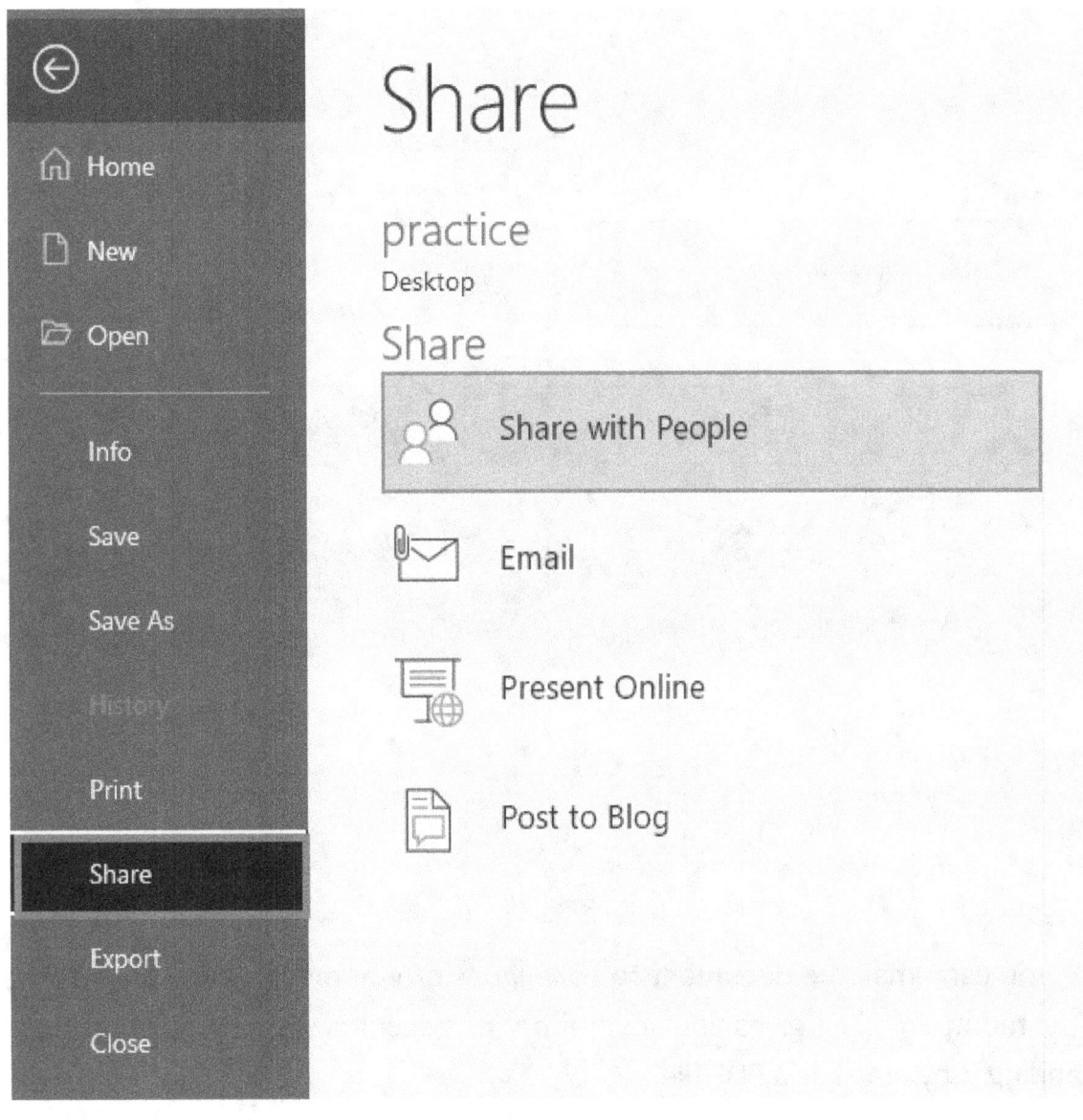

People usually share a document because they are in a team and collaborating on it. They also share documents to share information.

Microsoft Word gives you several options for sharing your documents.

You can share the document with people by saving it to the cloud and giving them the link to the document on the cloud.

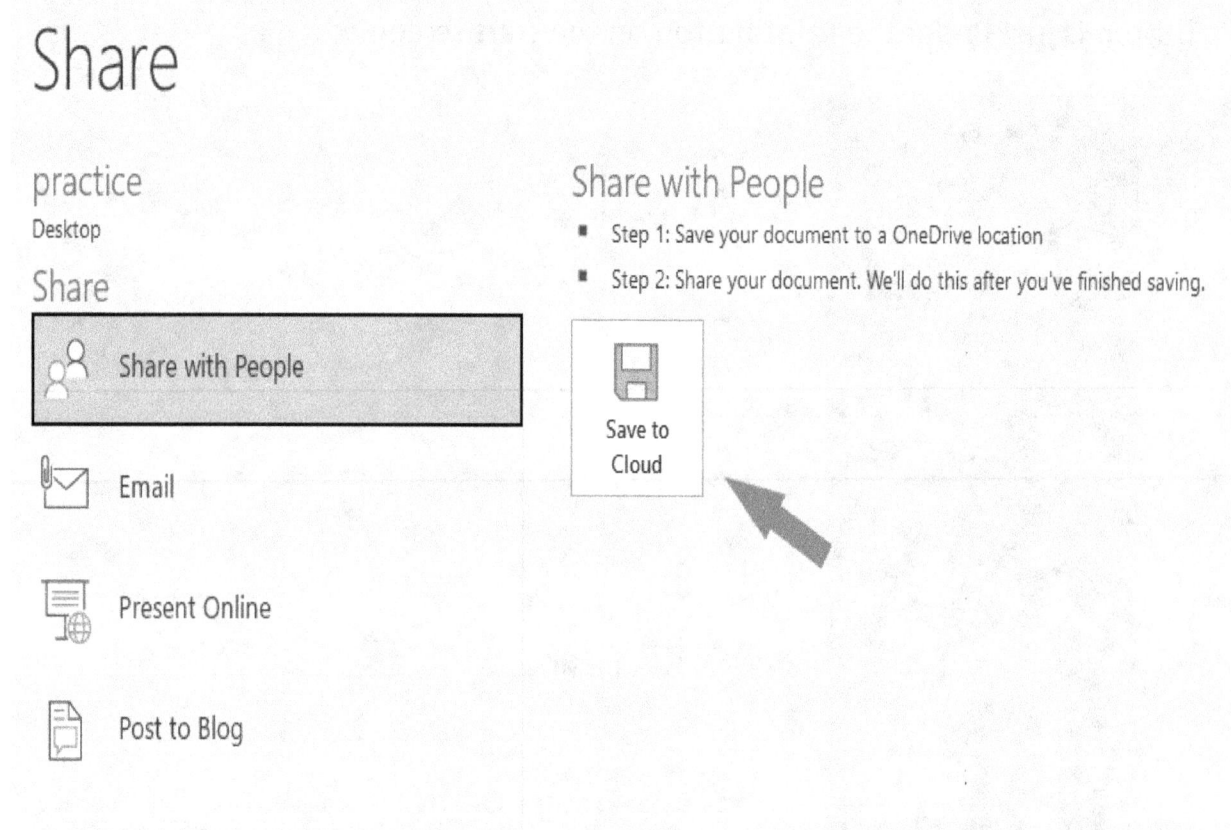

Or you can email the document to colleagues or whomever you want to receive the document. Emailing gives you several options such as sending as an attachment or sending it by email as a PDF file.

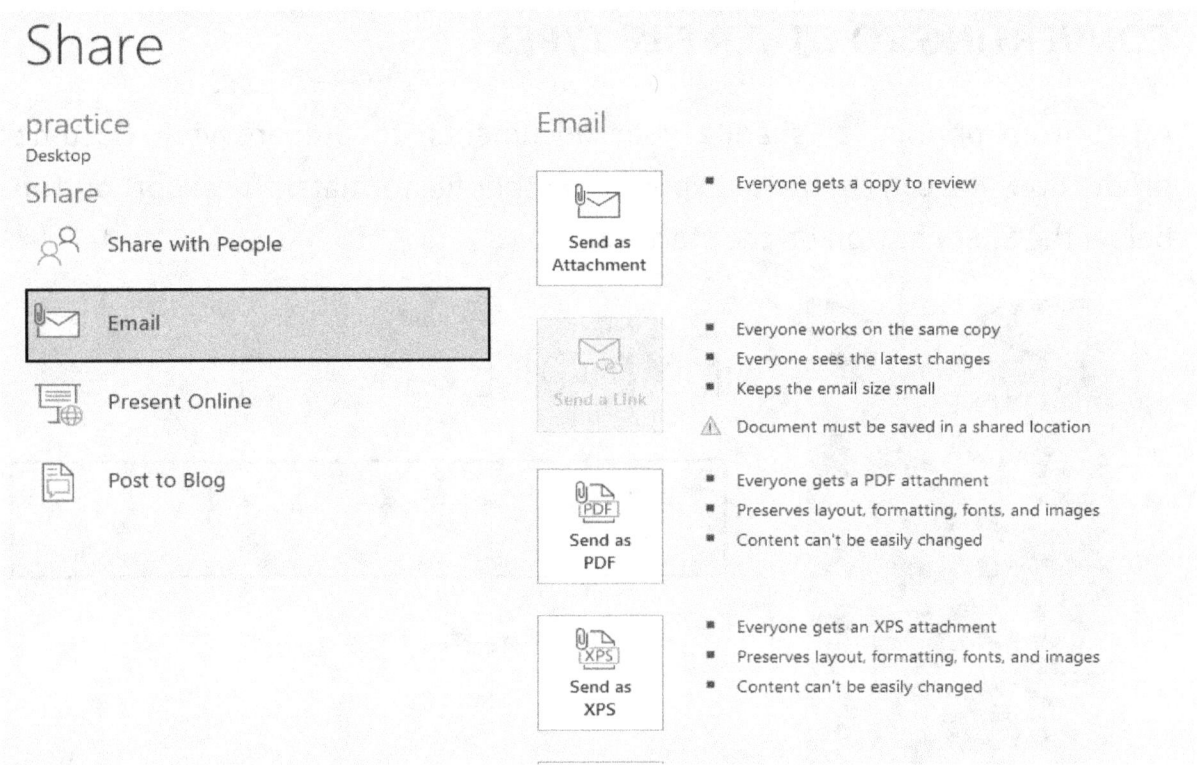

You can present the document online so that others can download it from the presentation.

Lastly, you can post to your blog.

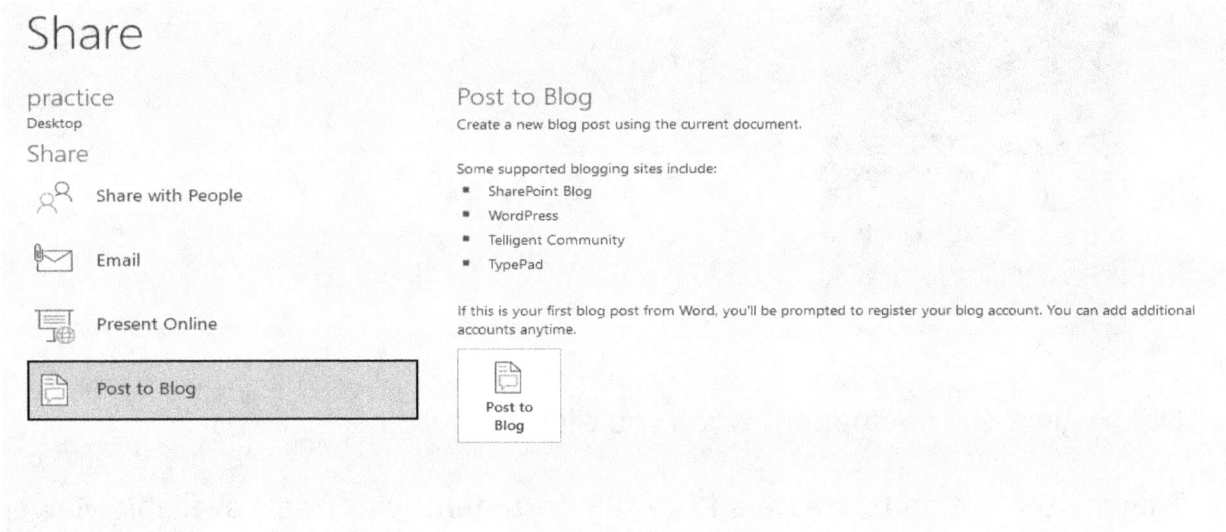

CONVERTING TO OTHER FILE TYPES

Apart from printing or sharing your documents, to prepare your document for production, you can choose to export it to other file formats. The export button is just below the Share button on the start screen.

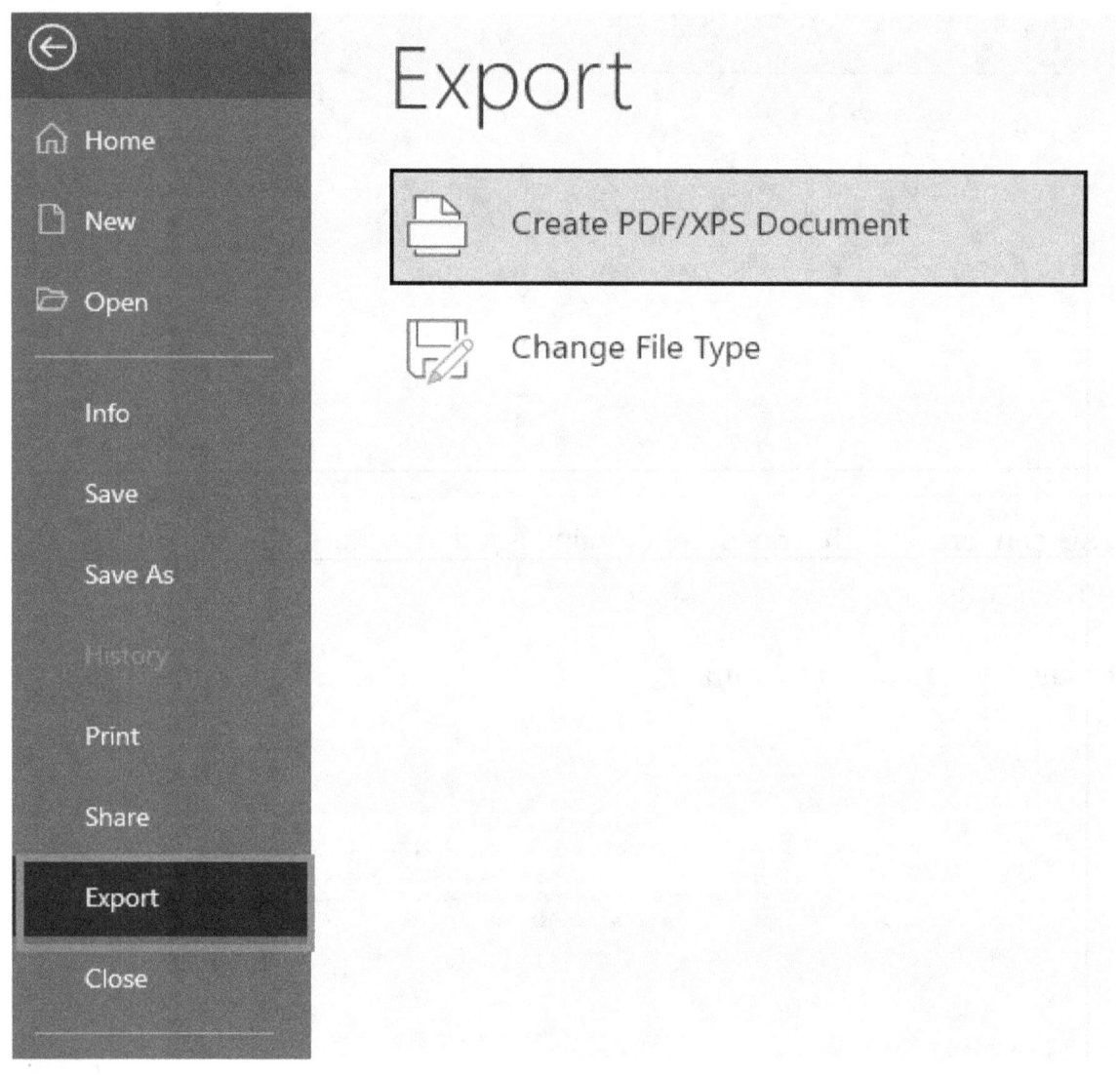

Export gives you two options when you click the button.

There is the option to **create a PDF/XPS document** with freely available viewers on the Internet. With this exporting option, the document's layout cannot be changed.

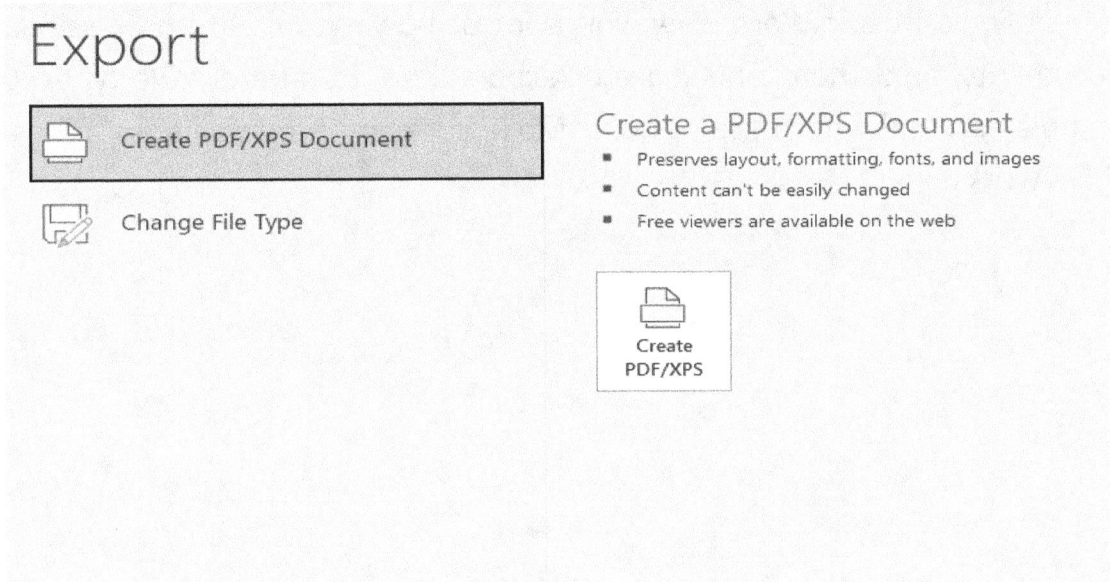

There is also the option to change the file type of the document. The **Change File Type** button gives you a wide range of options for converting your document to other file types. You can convert to a backward compatible **Document File Type** such as a **Word 97 - 2003 Document**, or to **Other File Types** such as a plain text file without any formatting and a rich text format (RTF). After you have chosen a file type, click the **Save As** button and the conversion occurs immediately.

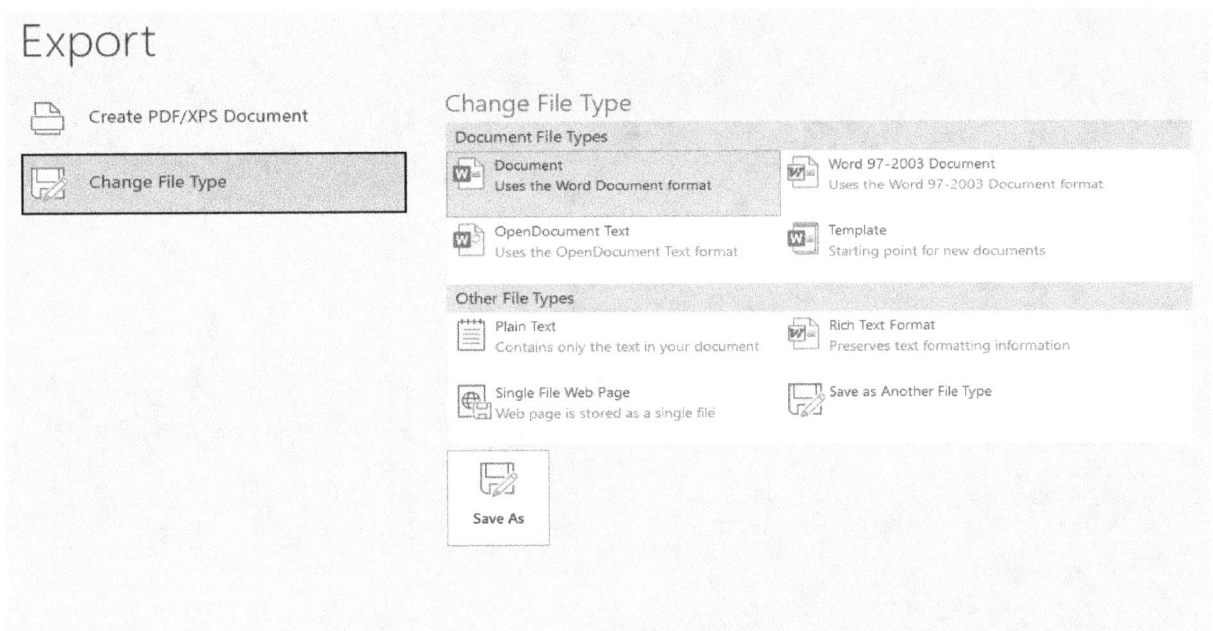

Evidently, Microsoft Word gives you a lot of power to create professional-looking documents, print them, and share or export them to different file types. Go ahead and play around with these options. Make sure you are familiar with how each of them works.

CONCLUSION

This is the last part of the **Microsoft Word For Beginners 2023** guide. Congratulations on getting to the end. It was fun taking a look at all the wonderful and basic features and functions that are on Microsoft Word.

We started by looking at the interface, accessing the quick access toolbar, and formatting some text. Then, we were also able to do paragraph formatting. We also discussed how we can work more efficiently using the format painter and applying some styles.

Also, we were able to create some lists, and we learned how to manage lists. We also inserted tables and images. I hope you now have a firm grasp on the different options you can use with images on Microsoft Word.

Then, we were able to control the page appearance of a document by changing the orientation, and the size and applying some background watermarks. We then looked at some of the proofing and review tools to prepare our documents.

Finally, we looked at how to publish our documents and share them with others. We converted our document to PDF and other formats.

It was fun spending time with you. From now on, you can be able to use Microsoft Word as a professional.

We also have other books, guides, and tutorials on other Microsoft products. I look forward to being with you as you increase your knowledge of handling the Microsoft suite of tools.

Thank you for choosing us.